1001
shocking
SCIENCE
FACTS

1001 shocking SCIENCE FACTS

A fiendish formula for fun...

Anne Rooney

ARCTURUS

ARCTURUS

This edition published in 2008 by Arcturus Publishing Limited
26/27 Bickels Yard, 151–153 Bermondsey Street,
London SE1 3HA

ISBN: 978-1-84858-008-4

Printed in Singapore

Author: Anne Rooney
The right of Anne Rooney to be identified as the author of this work
has been asserted under the Copyright, Designs and Patent Act, 1988.
The author can be contacted at anne@annerooney.co.uk

Design & Illustration by quadrum▪
Goblin illustrations by Steve Beaumont

Editor: Kate Overy

CONTENTS

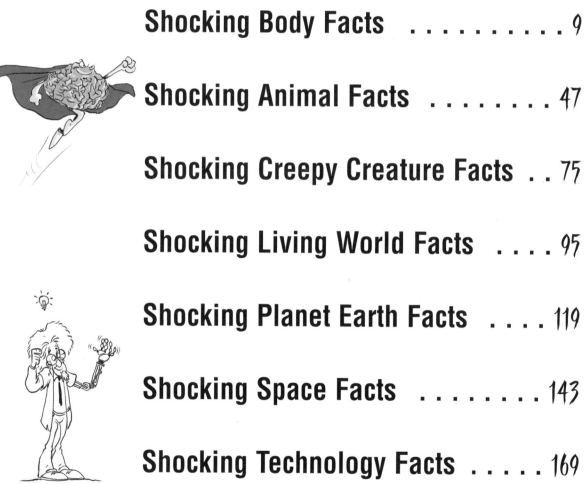

Prepare to be zapped!

Electricity isn't the only thing in science that's shocking. Some scientists experiment by digging around in rubbish dumps or poking through things that come out of the wrong end of animals! Others chase big, slithering worms that live inside your body or work with poisons so deadly, a single bottle could kill everyone on earth…let's hope they don't have gooey worm slime on their hands when they pick up the bottle! There are even scientists who watch dead bodies rot or send messages into space to try to talk to aliens for a living. It's no wonder we think of mad scientists and nutty professors – some of the things they get up to are truly shocking!

Science helps us to explore the world and the universe around us and it uncovers some pretty weird and wonderful stuff. But if you thought scientists knew everything, think again – we don't know what 97 per cent of the universe is made of! That means there's still plenty for you to discover, so get your lab coat on…and get experimenting!

Sports science

Even extreme sports like surfing, snowboarding and skydiving are fuelled by the power of science! Here are a few free skydiving facts (not part of your 1001 total) to get your heart racing!

Skydivers fall through the sky at speeds of 190 kilometres (120 miles) per hour! It's the force of gravity that pulls them back down to Earth.

As a skydiver falls, super-fast wind is slowed as it enters their airways to help them breathe. Oxygen is also absorbed through their skin.

Scientists developed a vertical wind tunnel that blows air upwards at huge speeds so that skydivers can have their fun indoors!

A formula for fun

Science really is amazing! Did you know there's a tree that cuts its own branches off? And a type of male fish that lives inside its female mate? Or that the land mammal with the most teeth doesn't actually use any of them? Do you know how long a lightning bolt is? How fast raindrops fall? Or which plant can live for 10,000 years?

No? Well, you're about to find out!

Don't do anything shocking...

If your hair is standing on end with excitement after reading all
the electrifying facts in this book, you might feel inspired to try
some experiments of your own! A word of advice...stick to
things like using laughter to combat your allergies, or keeping a
record of whether you've eaten a car's weight in food in a year!
Leave the truly shocking tests like drinking your own vomit to
all the mad scientists out there...

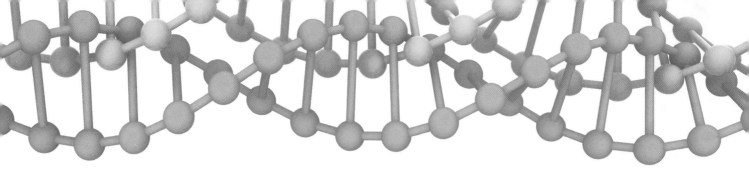

Shocking Body Facts

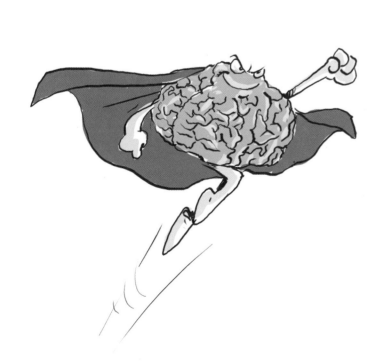

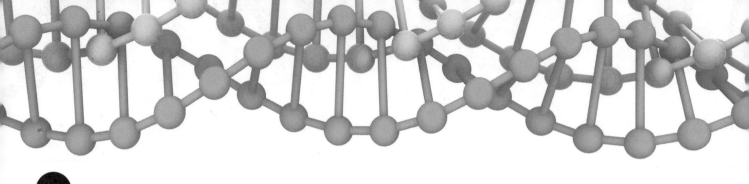

If a person is struck by lightning, they sometimes *vaporize* (evaporate) completely, so that there is nothing left of them at all.

Bacteria trapped inside a salt crystal for 250 million years were revived and grown by scientists in the USA.

An Anglo-American company will store samples of your disease-fighting white blood cells, so that more can be made if you get ill.

An adult human takes about 23,000 breaths per day.

It takes less than 0.1 grams (0.004 ounces) of poison found in parts of the pufferfish to kill an adult human. However, some people eat the fish regularly as they know which bits to remove!

Dead bodies can remain perfectly intact after many years. This can happen when fat in the body turns into a type of soap that doesn't rot.

Some people are 'human calculators' and can do really complicated sums in their heads instantly – even faster than someone with a calculator! No one knows exactly how their brains are different.

If scientists could build a brain from computer chips, it would take a million times as much power to run as a real human brain.

Malaria is a tropical disease spread by mosquitoes. Since the Stone Age, malaria has been responsible for half of all human deaths from illness.

Each person's tongue print is unique.

In ancient times, Indian doctors used live ants to 'stitch' wounds together. The doctor would hold the edges together and get the ant to bite through the skin. The ant's head would then be snapped off leaving its jaws as the 'stitch'!

Your brain receives about 100 million pieces of information at any one moment from your eyes, nose, ears, skin and receptors inside your body.

Eating asparagus produces a chemical that makes urine smell strongly, although not everyone can smell it. Lucky them!

A sneeze travels at 161 kilometres (100 miles) per hour.

A body left unburied in a tropical climate will be reduced to a skeleton in two weeks by the action of insects.

People can be born with ears growing from their necks or chests.

There are more bacteria in your mouth than there are people in the whole world!

More people are allergic to cows' milk than to any other food or drink.

Rubbing yourself with a garlic clove is supposed to keep mosquitoes away... and vampires... and probably other people, too!

People are taller in the morning than in the evening. During the day, the weight of your body compresses your spine as you walk around, then when you are asleep it expands again.

Electrical activity is detectablein a human brain up to 37 hours after death, possibly caused by chemical reactions.

The spice nutmeg is harmless if eaten in moderation, but deadly poisonous if injected. Beware!

Your stomach lining replaces itself every three days.

If you could lay out all the possible nerve connections in your brain, end to end, they would stretch to about 3.2 million kilometres (2 million miles).

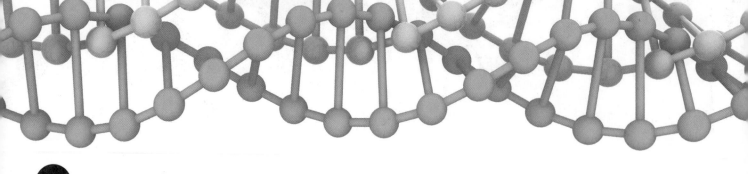

The strongest muscle in your body is your tongue!

If you read a novel that's 100,000 words long (about 300 pages) your eyes will travel just under 1 kilometre (more than half a mile) along the pages.

There have been many cases of people spontaneously bursting into flames and dying. Often, their whole body is burned away. No one knows exactly why this *spontaneous human combustion* happens. What a way to go!

Your eyes take about an hour to get accustomed to the dark, but after that they are 100,000 times as sensitive to light as they are in bright sunlight.

Your skin is shed and regrown about every 27 days. Most people get through around 1,000 skins in a lifetime.

There is enough acid in the human digestive system to dissolve an iron nail completely.

Your body destroys or loses two and a half million red blood cells every second. Luckily, it creates more at the same rate!

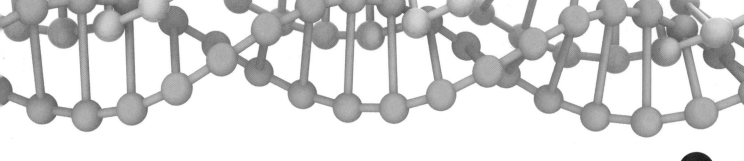

Beard hair grows faster than any other hair on the human body. If left to grow for his whole life, a man's beard could be 9 metres (30 feet) long.

There is enough iron in your body to make a nail...which you could then dissolve in all the acid!

Women blink twice as often as men.

The *placenta,* which nourishes an unborn baby, is the only organ that develops after a person is fully grown. It is lost when the baby is born and another grows if the woman becomes pregnant again.

One in 512,000 births results in triplets.

Only a few hundred people in the world are known to have the rare blood type H-H. A person with H-H blood can't receive blood transfusions of any other blood type and may need to store their own blood in advance of an operation.

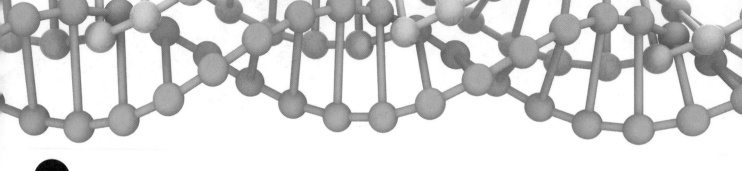

When you hold a seashell to your ear to 'hear the sea', what you actually hear is your own blood in the blood vessels of your ear.

If you could join up all the eyelashes you will lose during your lifetime they would stretch to about 30 metres (100 feet).

People who have lost a limb in an accident or operation often feel pain or itching in it, even though it's no longer there...

Hair grows most quickly during the day in the summertime. It grows more slowly at night and in winter.

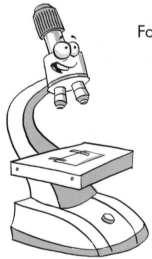

For years, doctors thought the appendix in the gut didn't do anything. But in 2007, scientists discovered that it helps to grow new helpful bacteria if vital bacteria in the gut are killed by illness.

If all the blood vessels from a human body were laid end to end they would stretch 97,000 kilometres (60,000 miles).

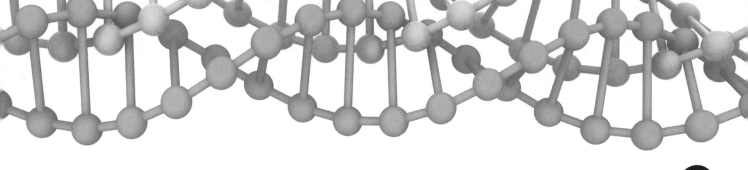

A single human hair can support the weight of an apple.

You lose around two billion skin cells every day, which adds up to around 2 kilograms (4.5 pounds) in a year.

Everyone spent about half an hour of their life as a single cell, at the start of their mother's pregnancy.

A chemical found in asparagus attracts fish. During the First World War, American soldiers were issued with asparagus so that if they were stranded near water they could eat the asparagus, urinate in the water and catch some fish to eat!

If you rubbed garlic on the bottom of your foot, it would be absorbed through your skin and eventually your breath would smell of garlic!

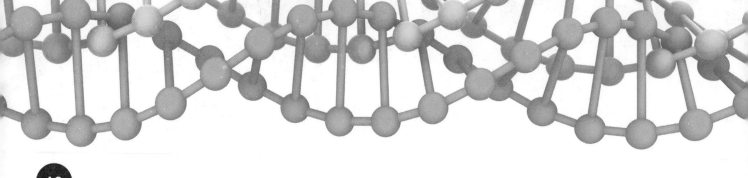

Laughing seems to reduce a person's allergic responses. So if you have hay fever, try laughing about it!

Around 10 per cent of the population is left-handed, but boys are one and a half times more likely to be left-handed than girls.

The bad smell of faeces comes from chemicals produced by bacteria that break down the food in your gut.

Your brain gets lighter as you get older. In your twenties, it starts to lose up to a gram (0.035 ounces) a year as cells die and are not replaced.

Girls have more taste buds than boys.

Even though some dreams seem to last ages while you are experiencing them, they generally only take about 2-3 seconds. Most people have at least seven dreams a night.

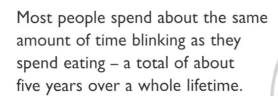

Most people spend about the same amount of time blinking as they spend eating – a total of about five years over a whole lifetime.

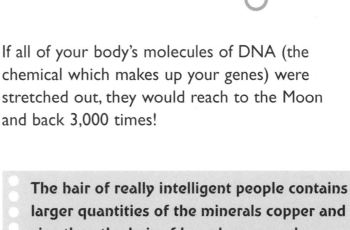

The world record for holding your breath is 7.5 minutes. Most people can only manage around 1 minute.

The heat output from the average adult body is enough to boil 30 litres (around 53 pints) of freezing water.

If all of your body's molecules of DNA (the chemical which makes up your genes) were stretched out, they would reach to the Moon and back 3,000 times!

The hair of really intelligent people contains larger quantities of the minerals copper and zinc than the hair of less clever people.

It is impossible to sneeze with your eyes open.

When you sneeze, all of your bodily functions stop momentarily.

An average person falls asleep in seven minutes.

Being cold in the night tends to give you bad dreams. The colder the room, the more likely you are to have a bad dream. Wrap up warm tonight!

If you have your head cut off, you may remain conscious and able to see for several seconds before you die.

About 125 grams (5 ounces) of the food you eat each day comes out as faeces. Most of the rest is water, and the remainder is nutrients absorbed by your body.

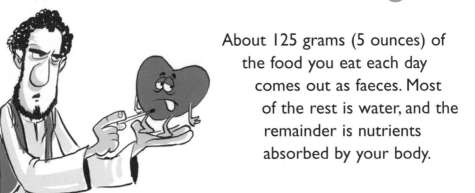

In the 1930s, it was not uncommon for women to swallow live tapeworms in an attempt to lose weight. The tapeworms would live in their stomachs, eating some of the food the women ate.

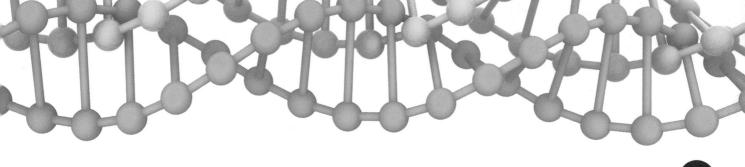

Your fingernails grow four times faster than your toenails.

It only takes about 10 days to die from a total lack of sleep.

People who live at very high altitudes have blood in their bodies that can deliver oxygen around the body much more efficiently than the blood of sea-level dwellers.

Dripping concentrated chilli oil into open wounds during surgery numbs the nerves for weeks and prevents patients feeling pain after an operation.

Chewing bread or gum while you peel onions will prevent the onions making you cry.

A 'body farm' is a research centre where dead bodies are left to decay in various situations. Scientists study their decomposition and the information is used to help police with murder investigations.

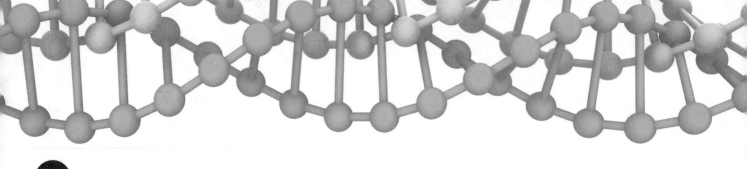

Mitochondria are parts of the cells in our bodies. Scientists think that they were originally bacteria, which have become absorbed into our bodies and are now an essential part of us. They take in nutrients and make energy for our cells.

Chinese scientists are testing robot-controlled mice. They follow instructions from a computer transmitted through electrodes in their brains. Scientists are hoping to use their techniques to cure disabilities by bypassing damaged nerves.

Some substances colour your urine – if you eat lots of rhubarb, your urine will be orange, and blackberries can make it go red!

In 1804, trainee doctor Stubbins Firth tried to prove that *yellow fever* is not an infectious disease by drinking his patients' vomit! Although he did not get yellow fever, he was wrong. It is very contagious, but must enter directly through the bloodstream.

People in Pakistan have been visiting the dentist for 9,000 years. Archaeologists have found drilled and capped teeth in ancient skeletons discovered there.

Most people's ears grow a quarter of a centimetre (0.1 inches) per year for their whole life.

Genetic evidence shows that most people in Britain are descended from the Spanish. It's thought that Spanish fishermen colonized Britain 6,000 years ago and took over from the native Britons.

Most American fashion models are thinner than 98 per cent of American women.

The amount of electrical energy generated by your brain is enough to power a light bulb!

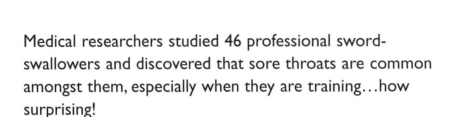

Medical researchers studied 46 professional sword-swallowers and discovered that sore throats are common amongst them, especially when they are training…how surprising!

Researchers think girls like pink and red colours because thousands of years ago their job was to hunt for ripe berries. Over the years girls' eyes became conditioned to seek out those berry colours.

Babies have many more taste buds than adults.

A chemical from bullfrogs may help doctors to wipe out the deadly MRSA virus, which infects some hospital patients. Frog chemicals have been used to treat wounds for centuries.

Neanderthal (early) man had larger brains than people have now!

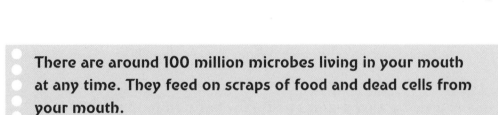

There are around 100 million microbes living in your mouth at any time. They feed on scraps of food and dead cells from your mouth.

One of our closest relatives is the *colugo* or 'flying lemur'. It's like a squirrel with bat-like flaps of skin between its arms, legs and tail and it glides from tree to tree. After apes, it's the animal genetically closest to humans!

One in 20 people has an extra rib.

Doctors in the old days used leeches to remove people's blood. Today, doctors still use leeches in some surgical procedures, as they produce chemicals that kill pain and keep blood flowing without clotting.

Gnathostoma spinigerum is a parasitic worm that lives under the skin. It moves around at a rate of about 1 centimetre (0.4 inches) per hour, so if you have one you can watch it moving under your skin!

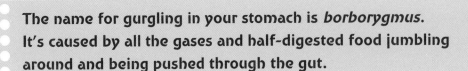

The name for gurgling in your stomach is *borborygmus*. It's caused by all the gases and half-digested food jumbling around and being pushed through the gut.

Gas you take in with food takes between 30 and 45 minutes to be released as a fart. It can come out quicker as a burp.

Dandruff is made of clumps of dead skin cells mixed with dirt and oil from your scalp. You lose millions of skin cells each day, so there's plenty available to make dandruff!

There are 2,000 glands in your ear that produce earwax. The sticky wax collects dirt, dead bugs and old skin cells before it falls out of your ears. It also kills germs!

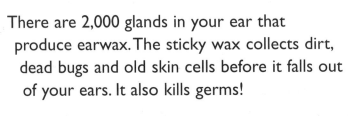

The water in urine comes from your blood. It goes from your food and drink through the gut wall into the blood, and is taken from the blood to make urine.

Mucous (slime) in your nose collects all the dirt you breathe in, including particles of smoke, pollen, exhaust fumes – and even dust from outer space! The slime and dirt clump together to make bogeys.

A pimple appears when a hair follicle becomes clogged by dried-up oil that oozes out of the skin.

Half of the bulk of faeces is bacteria.

Bile is the liquid that breaks down starches in your body. It determines the colour of urine, faeces and vomit.

Sweat only smells bad because bacteria break it down when it stays on your skin. So, if your armpits or feet smell, it's rotting sweat helped along by colonies of bacteria.

The broad tapeworm can live in your gut for decades and grow to 10 metres (39 feet) in length. You may not even know you have one…

There are tiny hairs all over your body, except for the palms of your hands and the soles of your feet.

In the condition *myiasis*, maggots hatch out and live under the skin – they can even be seen wriggling around. In 1993, doctors in Boston, USA, developed a treatment for myiasis that involved covering the skin with bacon. Maggots like the bacon, so come up towards it. Doctors then pull them out with tweezers. Gross!

Most people pass about a litre (2 pints) of gas a day as burps and farts.

Bacteria can survive 10,000 times the dose of radiation that would kill a person.

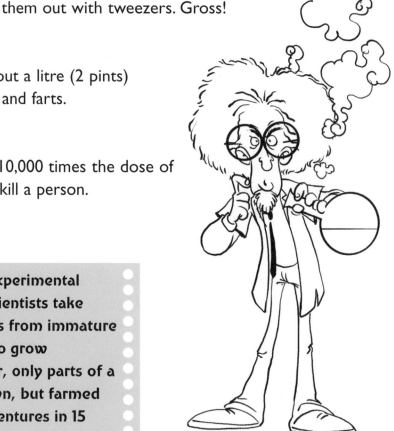

Tooth farming is an experimental technique in which scientists take dental *stem cells* (cells from immature teeth) and use them to grow complete teeth. So far, only parts of a tooth have been grown, but farmed teeth might replace dentures in 15 years' time.

Forensic scientists examine maggots and beetles eating dead bodies to try to work out the time that the person died. They work out at which stages of decomposition the different bugs like to eat the body.

Your stomach uses *hydrochloric* acid to digest your food, but if you spill it on to your skin, it burns you. The stomach produces mucous to protect itself from the acid. When someone dies and the mucous stops, the acid starts to dissolve the stomach.

When you vomit, the muscles that usually push the food down through your gut go into reverse and push it up and out of your mouth.

Dead bodies swell up as they rot, because decomposition produces lots of gas. Some dead bodies burp or fart as they release gas, which can be quite alarming!

There are several medical conditions that lead people to act like or believe they are wild animals such as wolves. These may explain some of the stories about werewolves.

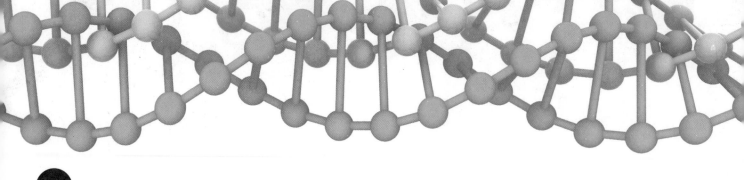

Roy Sullivan of the USA survived being struck by lightning seven times and eventually committed suicide.

Putrescine, one of the smelly chemicals produced by rotting dead bodies, is also partly responsible for bad breath.

You produce about a litre (about 2 pints) of saliva every day. It helps to break down your food before you swallow it, and to keep your teeth clean.

Some people pay to have their bodies frozen after death in case scientists work out a way to bring them back in the future!

When people die in extreme circumstances their muscles can go into spasm and freeze in their final position. Forensic scientists can use this to show that someone was still alive when pushed into a river, for example, or died holding a weapon.

Fleas that live on rats spread *bubonic plague,* which killed around a third of the population of Europe in the 14th century. They only started to bite humans because all the rats died.

The human body uses 60 calories an hour just to sleep – the same as it takes to watch TV. So if you were a complete couch potato, you would need to eat only 1440 calories a day.

The *placenta* (the organ which grows to nourish a baby inside its mother) uses the same biological tricks as a parasitic worm to hide from the mother's immune system. Without it, the mother's body would reject the baby as an intruder.

A blackhead is black because the oily gunk in it changes to a black colour on exposure to the air.

If a wound gets infected, find some maggots to put on it! They will eat all the rotten flesh and protect you from gangrene.

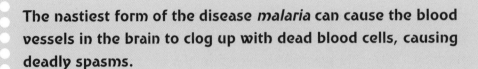

The nastiest form of the disease *malaria* can cause the blood vessels in the brain to clog up with dead blood cells, causing deadly spasms.

In the First World War, soldiers used the super-absorbent *sphagnum moss* to bandage their wounds. It can soak up four times as much blood as cotton bandages, but was a disgusting colour, like dried pus!

The human body contains an amazing 10,000,000,000,000,000,000,000,000,000 atoms.

Scientists have recreated the deadly flu virus that killed one per cent of the entire world population between 1918 and 1919. Smart, huh?

You will probably produce enough saliva during your life to fill two swimming pools.

A virus can only survive in a living host cell so it's not in a virus's interest to kill you. Even so, viruses caused all pandemic illnesses except bubonic plague, so don't get too relaxed about them!

Early anatomists were not allowed to study dead bodies, so they paid grave robbers to steal them. Often, the bodies of executed criminals were stolen and sold.

A flea carrying bubonic plague gets blocked up with plague bacteria then vomits them up into the bite it makes in its animal host.

If you don't have enough water, eventually your lips shrivel and go black, your tongue swells so that it won't fit in your mouth, and you can go nearly deaf and blind. Your skin turns grey or purple, your breath stinks and your spit turns gluey and smelly, and if you cut yourself you don't bleed. So make sure you drink up!

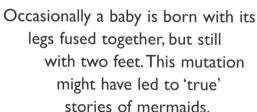

Occasionally a baby is born with its legs fused together, but still with two feet. This mutation might have led to 'true' stories of mermaids.

Casper's Law of decomposition states that a body left in the open air decomposes twice as fast as if it were immersed in water and eight times faster than if it were buried underground.

Xenographic transplants involve taking an organ from an animal and using it in a human being – a chimpanzee heart was transplanted into a man in Mississippi, USA in 1964, but the patient died two hours later.

The human stomach can hold up to 4 litres (7 pints) of partly-digested food. A cow's stomach can hold ten times as much – enough to fill a whole bath!

People who suffer from *migraines* (terrible headaches with sickness) have thicker brains than people who don't. Scientists don't know which came first in sufferers, the thickening or the migraines.

Stone Age people used to practise *trepanning* – an early medical procedure that involved drilling a hole in the skull. They had no anaesthetics, so it must have hurt – but the patients didn't all die – lots of skulls have been found with partly healed holes!

Many cures used in ancient times really do work. One was to put honey on wounds and then dress them with willow bark. Honey is an antiseptic, which stops the wound going bad and willow contains the same painkiller that's in aspirin. Genius!

A new way of treating cancer involves blowing bubbles inside the body. When the bubbles burst, they release heat, which kills the cancer cells.

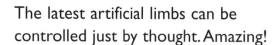

The latest artificial limbs can be controlled just by thought. Amazing!

Bacterial farms are used to produce certain drugs. Scientists have adapted bacteria to manufacture the hormone *insulin* needed by people with diabetes. Previously, insulin was taken from cows and pigs.

The human brain contains one hundred billion nerve cells.

A new method of transferring information, using the human body to carry the signal, means we could soon be able to pass on material such as photos and songs just by shaking hands!

Your nose and ears never stop growing.

Synaesthesia is a condition that jumbles up how people sense things. They might 'see' sounds as colours, or 'hear' smells as sounds.

Heavier women produce brainier children! Scientists believe that fat stored on a woman's hips contains acids that are essential to the development of the unborn baby's brain.

You're more likely to get ill from kissing another person than a dog. Even though a dog's mouth has as many germs as a human's, not as many of them are harmful to us.

A rare response to a virus that normally causes warts can also lead people to develop brown growths, which make them look as though they are covered with tree bark.

In one day, your blood travels 19,312 kilometres (12,000 miles)!

Before they are born, developing human babies have a tail, and some developing snake babies have legs. Perhaps we have more in common with snakes than we think!

It's possible that hiccups come from our distant ancestors who crawled out of swamps and had both lungs and gills. Hiccups may be a remnant of a way of closing off their lungs when in the water.

Your skin weighs about 3 kilograms (6.5 pounds) – the same as a bag of potatoes.

Most human mutations happen on the Y chromosome, which only men have.

People in some countries would bind their babies' heads using wooden boards, to make them grow into strange shapes...don't try it with your baby brother or sister!

A man born in England long ago had four eyes, arranged one pair above the other. He could close any one eye independently of the others.

Necrotizing fasciitis or the 'flesh-eating bug' causes your flesh to rot, die and fall off. It can be fatal, and even people who recover often lose whole chunks of their bodies. Yuk.

Zombies are not just a fictional invention. Witch doctors called *bokors* in Haiti, can use a special combination of plant-based drugs to make a person appear to be dead, then revive them and keep them under their control.

Being born with webbed hands or feet is quite common. It happens because fingers and toes develop from a flipper-like hand or foot that divides on the unborn baby. If it doesn't divide properly, the skin stays webbed.

Some people have an abnormality called 'hairy tongue' which gives them – you guessed it – a hairy tongue! In fact, it's not hair, but extra long *papillae* (the little bumps on your tongue). They also turn black!

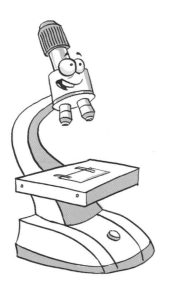

A Swiss journalist called Etienne Dumont is growing horns on his head. He has silicon implants under the skin and as the skin grows over them he replaces them with slightly larger ones.

Every year you will eat about 500 kilograms (1,100 pounds) of food. That's about the same weight as a small car!

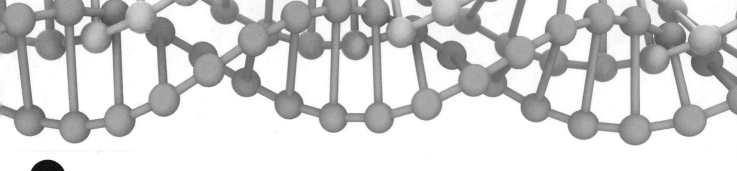

Even when you are elderly you will still have the tooth enamel that was formed in your mother's womb.

The skeleton of a body buried in PH neutral soil or sand can survive for thousands of years.

The skin of your eyelid is only 0.5 millimetres (0.02 inches) thick, the same width as a single hair.

Every day, you produce enough saliva in your mouth to fill five cups.

Humans can tell the difference between 10 million different colours.

A traditional treatment for the pain of arthritis is bee venom...but then you're faced with the pain of bee stings!

When girls are one and a half years old they are almost half their adult height. The same happens for boys when they are two.

When you look at your tongue first thing in the morning, it is covered in white stuff. These are cells that died during the night.

Forensic dentists examine teeth and tooth marks. Their work includes identifying dead bodies, and examining bite marks to match them to assailants.

In the 1700s a Russian woman had 69 children: 16 pairs of twins, 7 sets of triplets and 4 sets of quadruplets. That's a lot of birthdays to remember!

Carrots really do help you see in the dark – they contain vitamin A, which helps the retina to develop.

You have 10,000 taste buds on your tongue. By the time you are 60, half of these will have died.

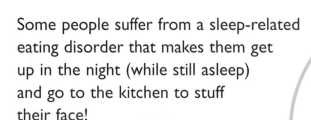

Some people suffer from a sleep-related eating disorder that makes them get up in the night (while still asleep) and go to the kitchen to stuff their face!

People who have been struck by lightning often develop musical ability they did not previously have!

Ebola fever is a horrible disease that makes people bleed from all their body openings, and turns their internal organs to liquid. Victims always die.

Human memory recalls events seven times faster than they really happen.

Many victims of the flu pandemic in 1918 went deep purple just before dying. Their lungs were so badly damaged by the disease that no oxygen could get into their blood.

You have more bacteria than human cells in your body.

Strychnine poisoning causes extreme muscle spasms. They can be so severe that the body can jerk backwards until the heels touch the back of the head and the face is drawn into a terrifying, wide, fixed grin.

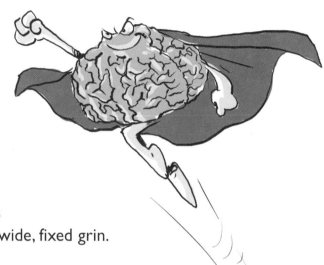

Messages are sent to your brain at around 360 kilometres (224 miles) per hour.

In 2002 German anatomist Gunther von Hagens carried out a public autopsy, cutting up a corpse in London, England. It was the first public autopsy for 170 years and was illegal. The police attended, but did not stop the autopsy or arrest von Hagens, and the autopsy was even broadcast on television.

Having hookworms inside your body can protect you from asthma. Some people have deliberately infested themselves with hookworm to get rid of their asthma.

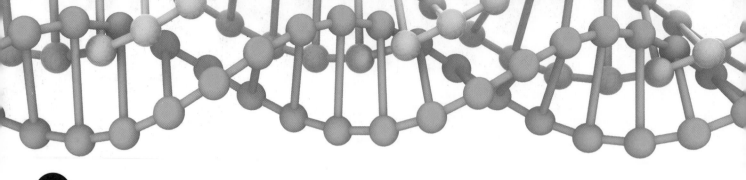

It is possible to die in just 4 minutes from choking or a blocked windpipe.

18th-century Italian scientist Lazzaro Spallanzani often made himself sick to get samples of stomach acid for his experiments.

The most dangerous animal to humans is the house fly – it carries more diseases than any other creature.

The human intestine is 9 metres (nearly 30 feet) long. Just as well it's all coiled up!

In 1822 a man called Alexis St Martin was shot in the stomach. A doctor called William Beaumont cared for him, but the wound didn't heal completely and the man was left with a hole leading right into his stomach. Beaumont used it to study the workings of the stomach. St Martin's meals used to leak out of the hole unless he kept it covered!

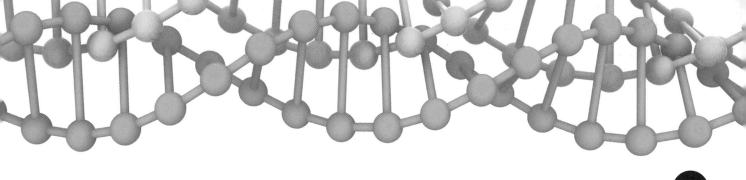

A Big Mac provides 2,365 kilojoules (565 calories) of energy. You'd need to cycle for 3 and a quarter hours to burn it off.

Some of the *Fore* people of New Guinea suffered from a strange illness that caused shaking, paralysis and death and defied medicine for years. It was eventually discovered that the disease, *kuru,* was caused by eating the undercooked brains of dead relatives, part of the Fore people's burial ritual.

Bodies buried in a peat bog may be naturally preserved for hundreds or even thousands of years. *Bog bodies* have dark leathery skin, but are still recognisable.

Your heart beats about 35 million times a year.

Hookworms enter through the feet, are carried in the blood to the lungs, and then travel up into the throat to be swallowed. The gut is their final destination – they bite onto it and live there.

An 11-year-old boy needs around 10,000 kilojoules (2,388 calories) of energy from food each day. A canary needs only 46 kilojoules (11 calories) and an elephant needs 385,000 (91,955 calories). The boy could get his 10,000 energy by eating 71 canaries or a small portion of elephant!

Bubonic plague has not gone away completely. An epidemic in Vietnam between 1965 and 1970 affected up to 175,000 people.

Anatomist Gunther Von Hagens offered to buy the body of Russian basketball player Alexander Sizonenko, who is 2.39 metres (7 feet 10 inches) tall, even though he was not dead at the time! Sizonenko refused.

People with the condition *Cotard syndrome* believe that they are already dead, and are walking corpses.

Shocking Animal Facts

In 1945, crocodiles killed 980 Japanese soldiers (of 1,000 in total) who entered a mangrove swamp to escape the British navy.

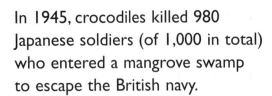

Polar bears have black skin underneath their white fur.

The *killifish* lives in temporary ponds in Venezuela. When the ponds dry up, the killifish embryos can survive in the mud, with no water or oxygen, for more than 60 days. No other creature can hold its breath for so long!

The *cosmopolitan sailfish* can swim faster than a cheetah can run! It can swim at least 109 kilometres (68 miles) per hour, while a cheetah can only manage 100 kilometres (62 miles) per hour.

In just over 100 years, the 'passenger pigeon' went from being the most common bird in the world (in 1810) to being extinct (in 1914).

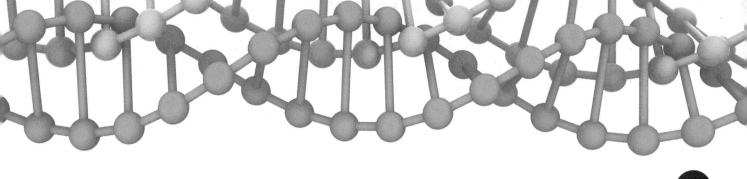

The blue whale has the slowest heartbeat of any animal
– it only beats four to eight times a minute.

Shaving a pregnant mouse makes her produce more milk
and grow larger babies. A bald mouse can digest more
food without overheating, and so makes more milk.

Some scientists believe that hidden
or 'silent' genes can return after
millions of years. A 'throw back'
happens if a silent gene gets turned
back on – making dolphins with legs,
for example, or people who are
as hairy as apes!

A rhino's rock-solid horn is made
of *keratin* – the same substance as
human hair, skin and nails.

Cats don't like walking across
aluminium foil – they hate the
noise it makes!

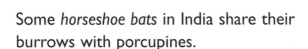

Some *horseshoe bats* in India share their burrows with porcupines.

Geese can fly up to 8 kilometres (5 miles) above the ground.

Bats always turn left when they come out of a cave.

The *vervain hummingbird* builds a nest half the size of a walnut shell and lays an egg that's only a centimetre (0.39 inches) long.

Savi's shrew (a tiny mouse-like mammal) is so small it uses the tunnels dug by large earthworms.

The largest *coprolite* (fossilized dinosaur faeces) measures 50 centimetres (19.6 inches) wide and was from a Tyrannosaurus rex more than 65 million years ago. It weighs 7 kilograms (15 pounds 6 ounces).

The only fruit eaten by aardvarks is called *aardvark cucumber*. The cucumber grows underground and relies on the aardvark to spread its seeds.

Giraffes have a special valve to help their hearts pump blood all the way up their long necks.

Elephants are the only animals with four knees.

Most hamsters blink with one eye at a time.

A porcupine can swallow 100 times the amount of poisonous *hydrogen cyanide* that is needed to kill a human and suffer no ill effects!

The emperor penguin can dive to depths of 534 metres (1,751 feet) – over one and a half times deeper than a human scuba diver can reach.

Rodents (such as rats and mice) make up 40 per cent of all mammal species on earth.

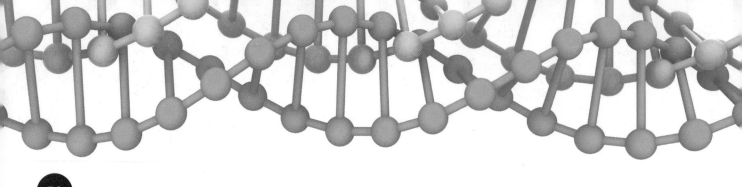

Sloths move so slowly that algae grows on their fur.

The *viperfish* impales creatures on its teeth by swimming straight at them. Its needle-like teeth are so large, they don't even fit in its mouth fully!

Fish can't chew.

A hyena can chew a broken bottle without hurting itself.

When staff at the British Museum saw the first *duck-billed platypus*, they thought it was a fake animal and tried to pull off its bill!

Walruses can get sunburnt! Other animals that can get sunburnt, (apart from humans) are light-coloured horses and pigs.

Woolly bats in West Africa live in spider webs.

The instinct to migrate is so ingrained in birds' bodies that even caged birds will turn and try to fly in the direction that they would naturally migrate. They do it at exactly the same time as wild birds, even though artificial light and heating should prevent them.

A cat is more likely to die if it falls from the top of a seven-storey building than if it falls from the top of a twenty-storey building. The extra falling time gives the cat a chance to realise what is happening and land properly.

The polar bear has the largest stomach capacity (in relation to its size) of any animal. It can kill and eat a large walrus or even a beluga whale.

The armadillo has more teeth than any other land mammal (around 100). However, it mostly gobbles up termites and ants, which don't need biting or chewing!

An anteater can eat 30,000 ants a day.

An African elephant kept in the New York Zoo had tusks that were 3.49 and 3.35 metres (11 feet 5 inches and 10 feet 11 inches) long!

Only ten per cent of the animal species that have ever existed are still alive today.

Using sonar equipment, scientists can detect the sounds made by fin whales and blue whales from 850 kilometres (350 miles) away.

The male elephant seal inflates its snout during mating. Once it's inflated, it can reach into its own mouth. Why would it need to suck its nose?

A cockerel that was inexpertly beheaded in 1945 lived for 18 months without its head! The farmer who owned the cockerel named him Mike, took him on tour and earned a small fortune!

A bird called the *bar-tailed godwit* migrates 11,500 kilometres (7,146 miles) from Alaska (near the North Pole) to New Zealand, flying non-stop. It loses up to 55 per cent of its body weight on the way.

Tigers have striped skin as well as striped fur.

Cats and dogs have sometimes travelled vast distances back to their original homes after their owners have moved house. No one knows how they do this so accurately.

The *star-nosed mole* can identify, capture and eat its prey in just over a tenth of a second.

An early ancestor of Tyrannosaurus rex is believed to have had feathery hair on its jaws and at the tip of its tail.

Tenrecs (Madagascan hedgehogs) are so greedy they often eat until they are sick.

The *hoatzin* is an unusual bird from South America. The chicks have claws on their wings, which they use to climb up trees!

The Egyptian vulture drops stones onto ostrich eggs to crack them, then eats the spilled eggs.

A kangaroo can't jump unless its tail is touching the ground.

The dinosaur *stegosaurus* was usually about 9 metres (30 feet) long and 4 metres (14 feet) tall, but its brain was only the size of a walnut!

Very occasionally, a chicken egg contains another complete egg inside it. This happens when an egg goes back up into a chicken, meets another egg on the way down and the second egg forms around the first one!

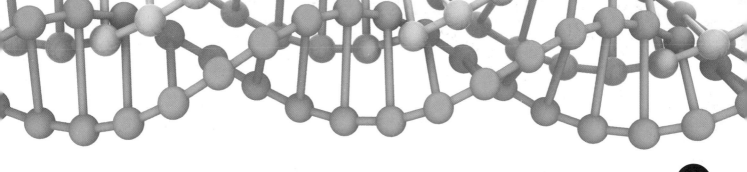

If a crow sees its reflection in a window it will sometimes fly straight at it repeatedly (even though it hurts itself on the window) as it thinks it is a rival crow. Birdbrain...

Rats can't be sick. Rat poison kills them effectively because they can't throw it up.

Giant flying squirrels have a 'parachute' made of a web of skin between their arms and legs. By spreading their limbs wide they can use it to glide between trees, covering a distance of 400 metres (1,310 feet) or more.

The ostrich has a small brain for its body size, making it one of the most stupid birds.

A giant bird like an emu that used to live in Australia between 15 million and 25,000 years ago stood 3 metres (10 feet) tall and weighed 500 kilograms (1,100 pounds)!

Meat-eating animals won't eat an animal that has been struck by lightning.

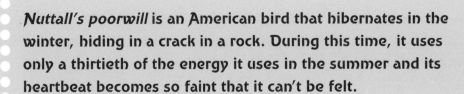

Nuttall's poorwill is an American bird that hibernates in the winter, hiding in a crack in a rock. During this time, it uses only a thirtieth of the energy it uses in the summer and its heartbeat becomes so faint that it can't be felt.

A hippopotamus has skin that's 3.5 centimetres (1.5 inches) thick – it's almost bullet proof!

A whale can carry up to 454 kilograms (1,000 pounds) of barnacles attached to its body.

The *Arctic tern* flies a round trip of 35,000 kilometres (21,750 miles) a year, breeding in the Arctic in the northern summer and feeding in the Antarctic during the southern summer.

Early explorers thought that a giraffe was a cross between a camel and a leopard and called it 'cameleopard'!

A Galapagos tortoise called Harriet (said to have been collected by Charles Darwin in 1835) lived at a zoo in Brisbane, Australia, until she died in 2006 – making her over 170 years old!

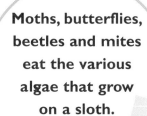

Moths, butterflies, beetles and mites eat the various algae that grow on a sloth.

The *sooty tern* can stay airborne for 10 years. It eats, drinks and sleeps while flying, and only lands to breed and rear its young.

An *albatross* can glide without flapping its wings for six days, given the right wind conditions.

The gigantic dinosaur, *Sauroposeidon* could stretch its neck up to 17 metres (55 feet).

When they are young, *flatfish* look like ordinary fish with an eye on each side. As they grow, one eye moves around so that both eyes are on the same side! The fish becomes wider and flatter and begins to live lying flat at the bottom of the sea.

Penguins can't fly but they can jump nearly 2 metres (6 feet) into the air.

The male *anglerfish* is much smaller than the female and spends most of his life attached to his mate's body. That's one way to keep your boyfriend in order!

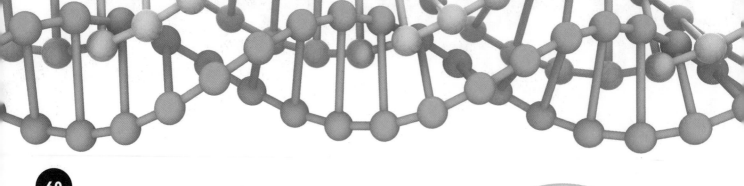

Whales can't move their eyeballs. To change the direction in which it is looking a whale has to move its entire body.

A pigeon's bones weigh less than its feathers.

Sharks have to keep swimming in order to keep water moving through their gills. If they stop, they will drown.

The *tailorbird* makes a nest from leaves that it stitches together. It punches holes in the leaves with its sharp bill, and then uses long grass to stitch them together.

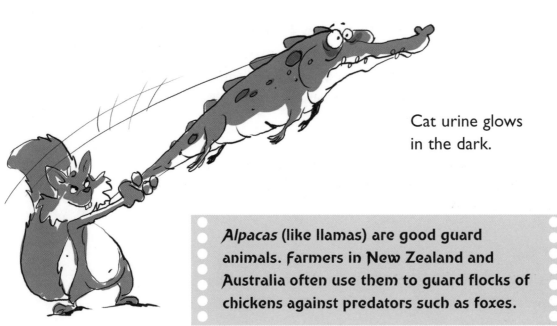

Cat urine glows in the dark.

Alpacas (like llamas) are good guard animals. Farmers in New Zealand and Australia often use them to guard flocks of chickens against predators such as foxes.

Items found inside the stomachs of sharks include a horse's head, a porcupine, parts of bicycles and cars, paintbrushes, a sheep, a chicken coop, and a suit of armour with the remains of a French soldier inside!

The fingerprints of koala bears are almost indistinguishable from those of humans.

Male seahorses become pregnant! The babies grow for three weeks in a pouch and then males give birth to up to 200 of them over 72 hours. The effort leaves him drained of colour – not surprising!

Piranhas have super-strong teeth that can bite through a steel fishing hook. They also have an unusual ability to detect the tiniest amounts of blood in water.

A shark will carry on feeding even when another shark is eating it! It will also eat parts of its own body that have been bitten or cut off.

Some octopuses have been known to remove the stings from jellyfish they have caught and use them as weapons.

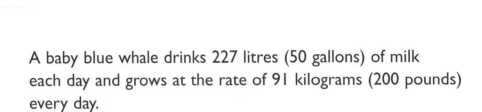

A baby blue whale drinks 227 litres (50 gallons) of milk each day and grows at the rate of 91 kilograms (200 pounds) every day.

Fish can be seasick.

A falcon can see an object that's only 10 centimetres (4 inches) long from 1.5 kilometres (about a mile) away. It can see clearly even when diving through the air at 160 kilometres (100 miles) per hour.

Goldfish are the only animals that can see in both ultraviolet and infrared light.

The duck-billed platypus can detect electric currents with its bill.

Elephants always walk on tiptoes, as there is no bone at the backs of their feet.

Some fish live so deep in the sea that it is permanently dark. Many make their own light by a process of *bioluminescence*, using chemical reactions to produce light.

A crocodile can't stick its tongue out.

The star-nosed mole has six times as many nerves going from its nose to its brain as a human has going from each hand to the brain.

Some sharks can detect the smell of fish at concentrations as low as one part in ten billion.

In May 1963, an American cow called Fawn was carried 0.8 kilometres (half a mile) by a tornado and landed safely in a field. Five years later, another tornado carried her over a bus!

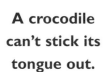

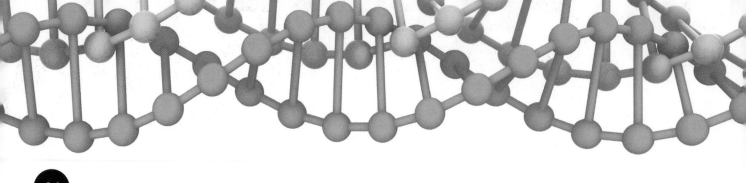

More than half of all creatures brought up from the deep sea by scientists are unknown species.

Reindeer are one of the few animals that can eat moss. It contains chemicals that help to keep their body fluids warm.

Cats can't taste sweet flavours.

Haddock never swim downwards. Fishing nets with holes at the bottom let dolphins and other things caught by accident escape, but haddock stay in the net!

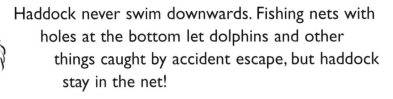

Buzzards (large birds of prey) can see small rodents on the ground from 4,500 metres (almost 15,000 feet) up in the air.

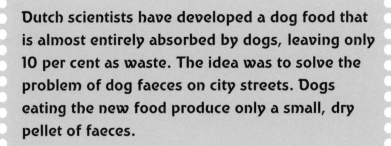

Dutch scientists have developed a dog food that is almost entirely absorbed by dogs, leaving only 10 per cent as waste. The idea was to solve the problem of dog faeces on city streets. Dogs eating the new food produce only a small, dry pellet of faeces.

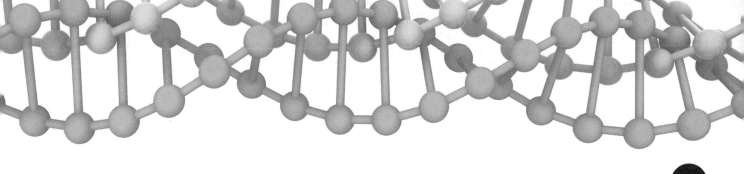

Guillemots are sea birds that roost in large groups. To help them tell their eggs apart, female guillemots lay eggs with very different patterns on the shells.

A donkey can look at all four of its feet at once.

Tuna never stop moving. They swim for their entire lives, covering a distance of around 1.6 million kilometres (1 million miles) over 15 years.

Some sea birds have red oil in their eyes, which acts as natural sunglasses to protect their eyes from the glare of bright sunlight.

Both chameleons and seahorses can move their eyes independently, so they can see in two directions at once.

When sloths go down to the ground once a week to go to the toilet, moths that live in their fur lay their eggs in the faeces – the larvae can then enjoy a delicious meal when they hatch.

A sperm whale can dive to depths of 2 kilometres (1.25 miles).

A goldfish kept in a completely dark room will eventually turn white.

Birds such as cuckoos and cowbirds lay their eggs in the nests of other birds. Some chicks have a hook on their jaw, which they use to remove the host chicks from the nest. The hook falls off when the chick is a few days old.

Scientists have discovered the remains of a dinosaur that was 1.8 metres (6 feet) long, tunnelled underground and lived in burrows – rather like a giant mole!

American scientist Robert Cornish carried out an experiment to try to bring animals back from the dead by moving their bodies up and down on a seesaw.

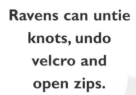

Ravens can untie knots, undo velcro and open zips.

In 1954, Russian scientist Vladimir Demikhov created a two-headed dog by grafting the head and front legs of a puppy onto a full-grown dog. The two heads would sometimes fight. The animal lived six days, but later he made one that lived a month. Freaky!

Scientists in Florida, USA, fitted an injured dolphin with a rubber tail after her real tail was amputated following an accident.

Albatrosses get seasick if kept on a boat.

Researchers at the University of Barcelona carried out a study, which showed that rats couldn't tell the difference between Japanese spoken backwards and Dutch spoken backwards. Maybe the rats just didn't care...

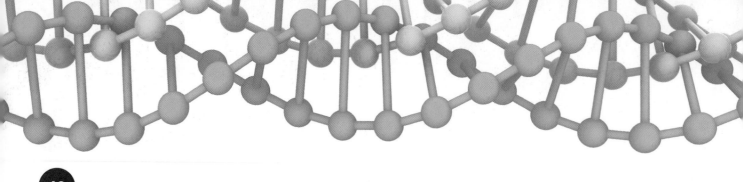

In 2001, a hammerhead shark in a zoo in Nebraska, USA, gave birth despite having no male partner. Some bony fish can also produce babies without a partner. The baby is a *clone* (an exact copy) of its mother.

The huge plant-eating dinosaur *diplodocus,* had a tail measuring up to 14 metres (45 feet) long.

A German aquarium plays love songs to its sharks in an attempt to get them to mate. The technique has also been tried with pandas and monkeys (but not in an aquarium!)

A giant panda can eat 45 kilograms (100 pounds) of bamboo in a single day.

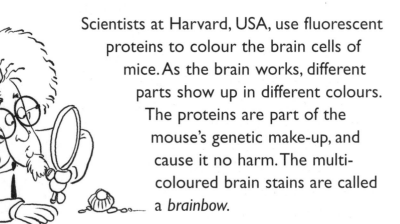

Scientists at Harvard, USA, use fluorescent proteins to colour the brain cells of mice. As the brain works, different parts show up in different colours. The proteins are part of the mouse's genetic make-up, and cause it no harm. The multi-coloured brain stains are called a *brainbow*.

Scientists using genetic engineering techniques have made a 'mighty mouse' that can run at 1.2 kilometres (0.75 miles) per hour for 4.8 kilometres (3 miles). It can live much longer than a normal mouse, and carries on having babies after a normal mouse would have died from the effect.

Tortoiseshell cats are usually female, but if they are born male, they're almost always sterile.

Homing pigeons use the Earth's magnetic field to help them find their way home.

The only animals that can recognise their own reflections in a mirror (besides humans) are the great apes, dolphins and elephants.

Swiss vets have found that dogs are suffering from stress more and more. Living in a city and having a demanding owner are two reasons dogs suffer from headaches, stomach pain and other stress-related symptoms.

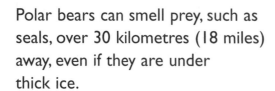

Polar bears can smell prey, such as seals, over 30 kilometres (18 miles) away, even if they are under thick ice.

A catfish has ten times as many taste buds as a human.

Some birds that lay their eggs in the nests of others revisit frequently to check up on their eggs. If their egg has been removed, they may have a strop and vandalize the nest, killing the other eggs or chicks.

An inventor in Sussex, England, designed a cat-flap that was colour-sensitive. It would let his ginger cat in, but not his neighbour's black cat. It was also linked to a satellite that he claimed could prevent nuclear war. At least the first part worked...

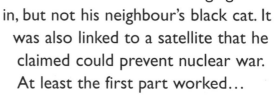

A toucan's tongue is shorter than its beak so it can't use it to help get food into its mouth.

A *tenrec* is a Madagascan hedgehog that looks rather like a spiky penguin. It can rattle its spines to scare predators and even detach some to leave as needles in anything that attacks it.

An Indonesian pig called the *babirusa* has long curved horns that grow up from its nose. In old animals, the horns sometimes grow in a complete circle and pierce the jaw. Not a good design!

The *matamata turtle* moves so slowly that algae grow on its shell. But when it eats, it sucks in large fish with a gulp so fast that it can't be seen with the naked eye!

A *starfish* doesn't have a brain.

Some tortoises urinate on their back legs to keep themselves cool in the desert. The evaporating water takes away body heat. But they must smell a bit!

Owls eat small animals such as shrews and mice whole. They then vomit up the bones and fur in compact pellets.

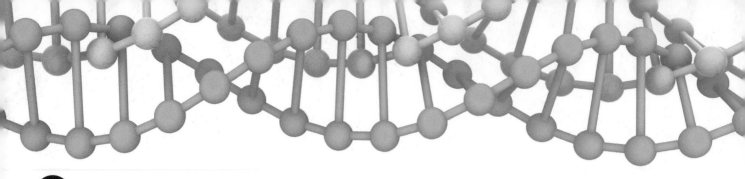

Sand grouse fathers have the tricky task of finding a drink for their babies in the desert. They fly to an oasis, up to 40 kilometres (25 miles) away, soak themselves in water, and then go back to the nest where the chicks drink the water from their feathers. Their belly feathers can only hold up to 25 millilitres (about a tablespoon) of water, so they have to make the round trip a few times!

Cows can go upstairs but not downstairs.

Some scientists believe that the first animals came from the sea, slithered onto dry land and grew legs and others did the opposite – they preferred the sea and so gave up their legs!

Zebras have individual striped patterns that are as distinctive as fingerprints.

Hummingbirds can't walk – they can only perch or fly.

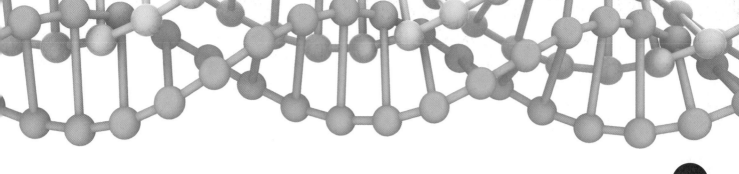

A dog has up to 150 square centimetres (23.25 square inches) of *olfactory membrane* – the area used to detect smells. A human has around 4 square centimetres (0.62 square inches).

Armadillos always give birth to *quadruplets* (four identical babies).

In a rare mutation, chick embryos can grow teeth like crocodiles.

Scientists sometimes pick apart *owl pellets* (undigested food that owls vomit out) to find out what they've been feeding on. You can even buy owl pellets to examine at home – so get some owl vomit and try it yourself! Eugh!

Elephants are the only mammals that can't jump.

A giraffe can lick inside its own ears.

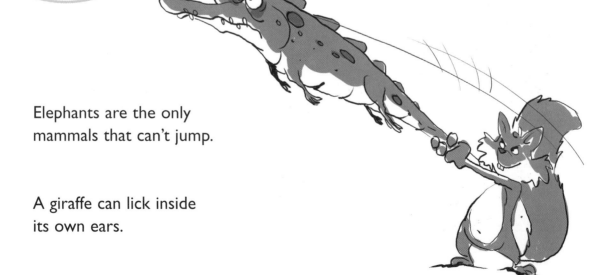

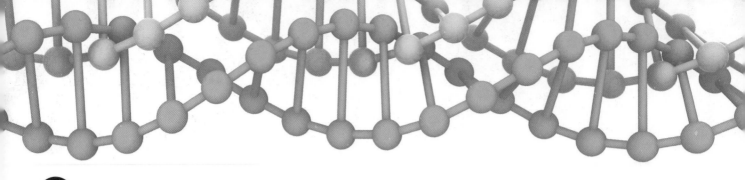

Farmers in Russia are farming moose for their milk. They use the scent of baby moose to try to tame the animals.

Porcupines float in water. (No, don't try it…!)

Whales sometimes beach themselves and get stranded on land, unable to move back into the sea. If one whale is stranded, its distress calls may bring others to help, leading to whole schools of whales being beached at once.

An octopus will eat itself if it becomes extremely stressed.

The hyena is the only wild animal that doesn't catch rabies.

Elephants have 40,000 muscles in their trunks which they can use to pick up a single blade of grass.

Shocking
Creepy Creature Facts

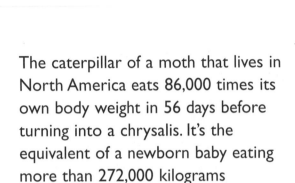

The caterpillar of a moth that lives in North America eats 86,000 times its own body weight in 56 days before turning into a chrysalis. It's the equivalent of a newborn baby eating more than 272,000 kilograms (600,000 pounds) of food!

Copepods are tiny crustaceans (like shrimp) that live in the sea. They are the only creatures known to have only one eye!

Moray eels have two sets of teeth in their throats. The first set of teeth bite onto an animal, then the second set move up into the eel's mouth, locking onto the prey. Finally, the first set of teeth move along the animal, dragging it into the eel's mouth.

The largest known spider was a *goliath bird-eating spider* found in Venezuela in 1965. It measured 28 centimetres (11 inches) across!

In just ten years, a poisonous spider called the *false widow* has colonized southern England. It arrived in bunches of bananas, and warm weather has allowed it to survive. There are now tens of thousands running wild!

The curly heaps of earth you find on the ground outside are worm casts – which are worm faeces.

The coconut crab lives on land and will drown if submerged in water. It grows to about 1 metre (39 inches) across and lives on islands around the Indian Ocean.

The vampire squid has eyes that make up an eleventh of its body length. It's as if a human had eyes the size of a table tennis bat!

Moths can emit their own high-frequency sound to stop bats from finding them…and eating them!

The total weight of all the earthworms in the USA is about fifty times the total weight of all the human beings who live there.

The slime produced by snails is so protectively slimy that a snail could crawl along the edge of a razor blade without cutting itself.

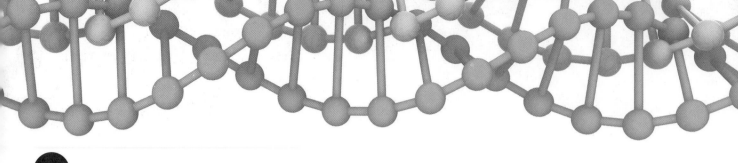

A rattlesnake's venom stays poisonous for up to 25 years after the rattlesnake has died.

Slugs have four noses.

In 1846 two desert snails were given to a museum. Staff assumed they were dead and glued them to a display board. Four years later they noticed one was still alive! After removal of the glue and a warm bath, it recovered!

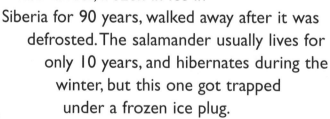

Lobsters carry on shedding their shells as they grow, eating the shells they have outgrown.

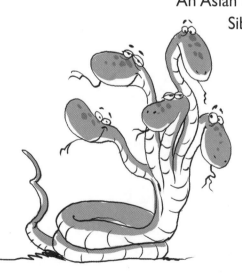

An Asian salamander, frozen in ice in Siberia for 90 years, walked away after it was defrosted. The salamander usually lives for only 10 years, and hibernates during the winter, but this one got trapped under a frozen ice plug.

A python can live for a year without eating a thing.

The *Polynesian skink* (a kind of lizard) has a bright blue tail. If the skink is attacked, it sheds its tail and runs away. The tail carries on wriggling after the skink has gone, keeping the predator distracted.

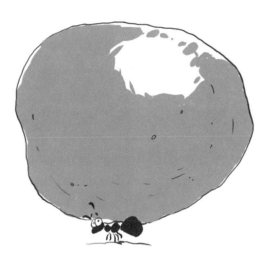

Ants can carry a load about 100 times their own body weight.

A chameleon's tongue is sometimes twice as long as its body.

A ribbon worm can eat 95 per cent of its own body without dying. It only does this if there is nothing else to eat.

The *paradoxical frog,* which lives in South America, is larger when it is a tadpole than when it is a full-grown frog! The adult frog is only ever about 6 centimetres (2.5 inches) long but the tadpole can grow to 25 centimetres (10 inches).

Leeches have 32 brains.

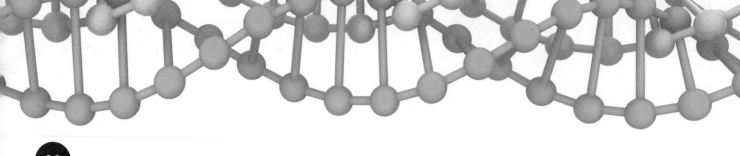

A type of deep-sea clam from the north Atlantic grows to a length of just 8 millimetres (1/3 of an inch) in 100 years.

In the Caribbean, there are tropical oysters and fish called *mudskippers,* which live in mangrove swamps and climb trees!

There are 100 million more insects on earth than there are humans.

A jellyfish is 95 per cent water.

A scorpion can withstand 200 times the amount of radiation needed to kill a human.

Wood frogs that live in the Arctic Circle can be frozen for several weeks of the year and then defrost, unharmed, when the weather warms up.

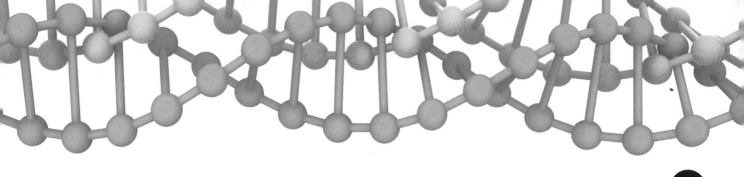

Honeybees communicate by dancing and moving their tails, but bees in different areas speak different languages!

Ten thousand new species of insect are discovered every year.

The light from six large fireflies is enough to read by.

An *aphid* (greenfly) gives birth to babies that already have their own babies formed inside them that are clones of themselves – they don't need to breed with a male. Over a whole summer a single aphid could give rise to 250 tonnes (551,155 pounds) of aphids.

Robber crabs eat coconuts. They grab onto the trees with their legs and climb up to 'steal' them.

The tarantula wasp will paralyse a tarantula spider and then lays its eggs in its live body. When the larvae hatch, they eat the spider alive!

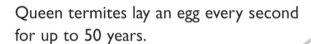

Queen termites lay an egg every second for up to 50 years.

Some types of baby spider in Australia bite the legs off their mother and eat them over several weeks.

If you spread out the tentacles of an Arctic jellyfish, they would stretch across 15 tennis courts.

Ants recognise other ants from the same colony by smell.

Insects eat 10 per cent of the world's food supply each year.

Occasionally, snakes are born with two heads. When this happens, the heads often fight each other for food.

A cockroach can detect movements as small as 2,000 times the diameter of a hydrogen atom.

An earthworm tastes with its whole body – it has taste receptors spread all over it.

A fly's eye has a flicker rate five times that of a human. A film made for a fly would therefore need five times as many frames per second as a normal film or the fly would see it as a series of still photos.

Mosquitoes are strongly attracted to people who have recently eaten bananas.

Mosquitoes are attracted to humans by the smell of their feet more than any other part of the body.

A scallop has about 100 eyes around the edge of its shell. This helps it to spot the shadow of an approaching predator.

The giant African land snail can grow to 39 centimetres (15 inches) and weigh 900 grams (2 pounds).

A baby lobster sheds its shell and grows a new one 35 times before hatching from its egg.

A grasshopper can jump 500 times its own height.

A cockroach can live for more than a week after its head has been cut off. Eventually, it starves to death.

Worker bees have 5,500 lenses in each eye.

Dragonflies are among the world's fastest creatures – some species can travel at about 48 kilometres (30 miles) per hour.

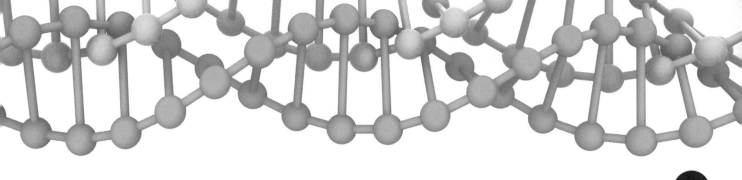

The silkworm moth can no longer be found in the wild.
It has been domesticated for so long that it can no longer fly.

When a frog is sick, it throws up its entire stomach, which then hangs out of its mouth. It uses its arms to scoop out the contents of the stomach and then swallows it again.

There are 35,000 species of spider but only 27 are known to be able to kill humans.

A leech doesn't need to eat often – cells from a meal enjoyed 18 months before can sometimes be found in its stomach.

Eighty per cent of all living things are *nematode worms* – simple worms found everywhere including salt and fresh water, soil, and inside plants and animals.

White's tree frog is pale green in the sunlight but turns white when it goes into the shade. It lives in trees – and toilet cisterns! It's often found in toilets in Australia and New Guinea.

Neither butterflies nor peacocks have any coloured pigments to give them their iridescent colours: both butterfly scales and peacock feathers are transparent, but reflect light to produce colours.

The largest known spider, the *megarachne,* was found as a fossil in Argentina. It was 50 centimetres (19.7 inches) across.

Blue lobsters are a mutation – around one in every two million lobsters is blue.

Butterflies that fly at night have ears on their wings so that they can listen out for bats and avoid becoming a bat-snack.

In 1915 a terrible plague of locusts in Jerusalem darkened the sky in the middle of the day, blocking out the sun. They ate everything and laid millions of eggs. Even though all men between 15 and 60 years old had to collect 5 kilograms (11 pounds) of eggs each to destroy, 99 per cent of those laid still hatched.

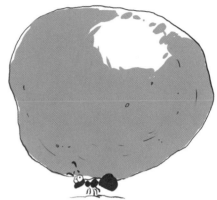

An ant has a larger brain for its body size than any other animal.

Roasted scorpions glow green under UV light.

Some species of deep sea squid squirt luminous ink instead of black! It creates a cloud of glowing light that distracts predators.

A housefly's feet are ten million times more sensitive to taste than a human tongue.

Cockroaches have been around for at least 300 million years – that's 100 million years before the dinosaurs evolved.

The total weight of all the ants in the world is roughly the same as the total weight of all the human beings in the world.

It would take 27,000 spider webs to make just 0.45 kilograms (1 pound) of web.

A sea slug can eat a *hyrdroid* (like an underwater stinging nettle) without being stung. The stinging chemical is absorbed into its skin and then stings anything that tries to eat the slug.

Crickets chirp at different rates according to the temperature. They are so accurate that the temperature can be calculated from the rate of their chirping – as long as the weather is warm enough for them to chirp at all.

A frog being sick was first observed when one was taken on a space flight.

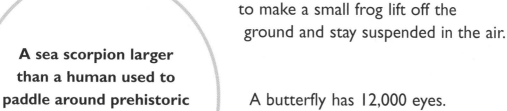

Using a powerful magnet, it is possible to make a small frog lift off the ground and stay suspended in the air.

A sea scorpion larger than a human used to paddle around prehistoric swamps 390 million years ago.

A butterfly has 12,000 eyes.

Tailor ants sew leaves together, not using a thorn or spike, but using their own grubs! They squeeze the grubs to get silk from their mouths, and pass them backwards and forward through holes in the leaves like a needle.

If a healthy earthworm is cut in half in the right place, it can grow a new head or tail. Of course, the worm might think there is no 'right place' to be cut in half!

Ants stretch when they wake up.

A *quahog clam* found off the coast of Iceland is between 405 and 410 years old, making it the oldest animal ever discovered. The clam has been named Ming by researchers. It was a baby when Elizabeth I was on the throne in England, and was already nearly 200 years old by the time of the French Revolution!

Ants can detect small movements through 5 centimetres (about 2 inches) of earth.

Dragonflies have almost 360 degree vision.

The *coelacanth* is a prehistoric fish which scientists thought had been extinct for 65 million years – until one was found alive and well in 1938!

Japanese scientists have bred completely see-through frogs so that they can investigate their internal organs without having to kill and dissect them.

The parasite, *toxoplasma,* prefers to live in cats' brains, but it can also infect rats, changing their brains so they are less scared of cats. This makes the rats more likely to be caught and eaten, allowing the parasite to move into the cat!

When they eat, *planarian worms* shoot a tube out of their throats to hold down their prey. They ooze enzymes out to soften the prey and then tear bits off it to eat.

Dragonflies can fly at up to 58 kilometres (36 miles) per hour.

A giant squid washed up in Canada in 1878 had a body that was 6 metres (20 feet) long with tentacles that measured up to 10.7 metres (35 feet) long.

Newts can re-grow body parts that are lost or damaged, including legs, eyes and even hearts. Scientists who have studied how they do this think they might be able to persuade human bodies to do the same.

If a cockroach loses a leg, it can grow another!

Copepods
(tiny crustaceans)
often live in groups
of up to a trillion
(1,000,000,000,000).

The *cusk eel* lives more than
8 kilometres (5 miles) below
the surface of the sea.

The *bombadier beetle* produces
tiny explosions – up to 500 a
second – which blast gases out
of its rear end to frighten
predators. The exploding farts sound
like a machine gun!

In Australia in 2000, a plague of 100 billion locusts
attacked wheat and barley crops.

Worms don't chew their
food – they swallow small
stones, which grind up the
leaves and other vegetable
matter they eat. Other
animals also keep stones
in their innards to break up
their food – even the
dinosaurs did it!

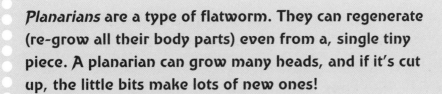

Planarians are a type of flatworm. They can regenerate (re-grow all their body parts) even from a, single tiny piece. A planarian can grow many heads, and if it's cut up, the little bits make lots of new ones!

A leech can suck five times its own body volume in blood at a single meal, in only 20 minutes.

An electric eel produces enough electricity to power two fridges!

The *glass frog* is lime green but has a completely transparent stomach. It's possible to see the blood vessels, the heart and even check whether it's eaten recently or might like a snack.

Crickets hear through their legs.

Leafcutter ants mix chewed-up leaves with spit and droppings to make yummy compost. They also grow fungus on their compost heaps to eat.

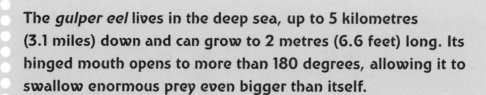

The *gulper eel* lives in the deep sea, up to 5 kilometres (3.1 miles) down and can grow to 2 metres (6.6 feet) long. Its hinged mouth opens to more than 180 degrees, allowing it to swallow enormous prey even bigger than itself.

The *darkling beetle* lives in the desert where it's hard to find a drink. It has a special method – it sticks its front end into the sand and leaves its back end sticking up at night. Fog condenses on its behind, then runs down the beetle's body into its mouth. Ingenious!

Oysters can change sex several times during their lives.

Scientist Laurence M Klauber (1883–1968) was known as 'Mr Rattlesnake'. He collected 35,000 pickled snakes and reptiles over his life. (He didn't eat them – they were pickled to preserve them for study!)

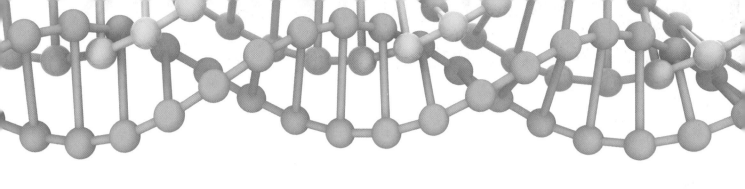

Shocking
Living World Facts

A mushroom from Africa, called *the Lady in the Veil,* grows faster than any other organism in the world. It grows up to 20 centimetres (8 inches) in only 20 minutes, and can be heard cracking as it grows!

There have been rainstorms with falling fish, frogs and toads!

Some trees communicate using chemicals. If a wood-eating bug attacks one, the tree releases chemicals into the air, which prompt other trees in the area to produce a poison that deters the bugs.

Rainforests cover a mere 2 per cent of the earth, yet more than half of all plant and animal species live there.

In 1894, a turtle that was frozen inside a giant hailstone fell to earth.

Trees grow from their tops – so if you carve your name into a tree when you (and the tree) are small it will still be at the same height when you are old.

A bacterium in spoiled food, which causes the food poisoning *botulism*, is one of the deadliest known poisons. Just 450 grams (one pound) of the bacteria could wipe out the human race.

Hot water freezes more quickly than cold water.

Lake Titicaca in Bolivia is home to lots of sea creatures – but it's an inland lake. The lake was stranded when the landscape changed, trapping sea creatures in its saltwater environment.

There was once a giant hailstone! In 1849 a block of ice that was 6 metres (20 feet) long fell from the sky in Scotland.

Parts of the Atacama Desert in Chile have had no rain for 400 years.

Some types of plants and animals have evolved to live in the most hostile places such as inside volcanic vents, at the bottom of vast caves, and even deep under the sea.

Ball lightning is the name given to fiery balls, that whiz through the air, lasting several seconds. No one knows what causes them and some scientists doubt they exist, even though there have been many sightings. In 1994, ball lightning left a hole in a closed window that measured 5 centimetres (2 inches)!

The South African *quiver* tree cuts its own branches off to preserve water. Clever tree!

There are about 10 million species of living things on earth.

Stinging nettles grow well in soil that contains dead bodies – they thrive on a chemical called *phosphorous* which is in the bones.

Water devils are small whirlwinds that make thin columns of water that whirl and twist over the surface of a lake. They can look like the neck of a monster, weaving to and fro, and might explain legends of beasts such as the Loch Ness Monster.

Old tales of a rain of blood can be explained by red sand being picked up, carried vast distances in clouds, and falling with the rain.

A rare herb that grows in Bolivia waits 80–150 years before it flowers.

Some clouds are up to 20,000 metres (65,000 feet) thick from top to bottom – nearly three times as tall as Mount Everest.

On 7th July 1987 the temperature in Kansas, USA, rose from 24 degrees Celsius to 35 degrees Celsius (75 to 95 degrees Fahrenheit) in just ten minutes!

A lightning bolt is five times hotter than the surface of the sun.

Potatoes are from the same family of plants as deadly nightshade. If the potato were to be discovered now, it would probably not be approved as a food!

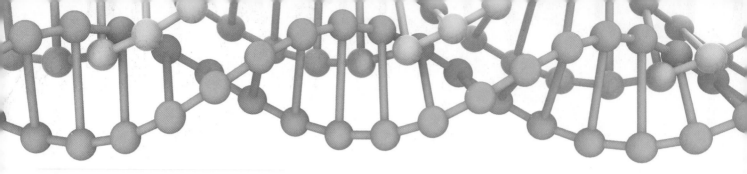

At any one time, around 100 lightning bolts are striking the earth.

A cactus that grows in the Arizona desert grows less than 2.5 centimetres (1 inch) in the first ten years of its life. It's a slow starter!

A litre (1.7 pints) of sand contains around 8 million grains.

The *corpse flower* or *stinking lily* is the smelliest flower in the world. Its stench is disgusting – it smells like a rotting corpse. This attracts insects that feed on the dead matter, and they pollinate the flower.

Some scientists estimate that up to two million species became extinct during the 20th century alone.

Don't believe the expression – lightning can, and does, strike twice! Tall buildings and mountaintops are especially vulnerable.

A *Norwegian spruce* pine tree growing on Campbell Island in Antarctica stands more than 222 kilometres (139 miles) away from the next nearest tree. It must be lonely!

In 1986, 92 people were killed in Bangladesh by hailstones that weighed over 1 kilogram (2.2 pounds) each.

A type of carnivorous plant found in the tropical rainforests of Asia can 'eat' birds and even rats. Animals are attracted by the nectar of the flower, and then fall into a vat of chemicals which dissolve them, feeding the plant.

A type of *amoeba* (single-celled organism) that lives in warm rivers, lakes and even swimming pools can infect people if the water gets up their nose. It eats their brain away and they die within two weeks. Although rare, death-by-amoeba is becoming more common! Scary!

Giant raindrops that were 8.6 millimetres (0.3 inches) across were measured in Brazil in 1995. The width of the drops was measured using lasers.

Some types of bamboo grow up to 91 centimetres (35 inches) a day. This means they are growing at a rate of 0.00003 kilometres (0.00002 miles) per hour!

Brazil is home to 30 per cent of the rainforest left on earth.

The *aurora borealis*, or Northern lights are displays of swirling green, red and other coloured light high in the night sky near the North Pole. They're caused by charged particles from the solar wind hitting atoms from the earth's atmosphere, making them emit coloured light.

Potatoes are the roots of the potato plant. They are where all the plant's energy is stored.

A *prickly cycad* (a type of plant) brought to Kew Gardens in London in 1775 is still alive, more than 230 years later.

In 1976, children playing in a school football match found their heads began to glow. It was an appearance of *St Elmo's fire* – a glow caused by the build-up of static electricity before a thunderstorm.

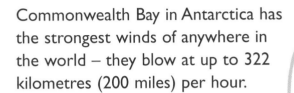

Commonwealth Bay in Antarctica has the strongest winds of anywhere in the world – they blow at up to 322 kilometres (200 miles) per hour.

It takes a tonne (2,204 pounds) of mulberry leaves, eaten by silkworms, to produce just 5 kilograms (11 pounds) of silk.

Tough little tadpoles of some species of frog are able to live inside a *pitcher plant* without being dissolved by its acidic juices.

The most poisonous plant in the world is the *castor bean*. Just 70 micrograms (2 millionths of an ounce) is enough to kill an adult human. It's 12,000 times more poisonous than rattlesnake venom.

The bark of the redwood tree can't burn. When there are wildfires in redwood forests, it is the inside of the tree that burns!

A *Venus flytrap* is a carnivorous plant that traps and eats flies. It doesn't strike quickly – it takes half an hour to squash a fly and kill it, and another ten days to digest it.

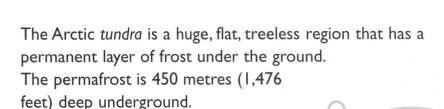

The Arctic *tundra* is a huge, flat, treeless region that has a permanent layer of frost under the ground. The permafrost is 450 metres (1,476 feet) deep underground.

The shell of a lobster is made of *chitin* – the same substance that mushrooms are made of.

The lily pads of a giant water lily that grows in the Amazon are strong enough for a small child to sit on.

Most bacteria are tiny – there can be 50 million bacteria in a single drop of liquid. Yet the largest bacterium can just about be seen with the naked eye.

The oceans provide 99 per cent of the habitable space on earth because they are so deep – on land, all plant and animal life is clustered on the surface.

Between the year 2000 and 2005, 80,467 square kilometres (31,068 square miles) of rainforest were lost to *deforestation* (cutting down trees).

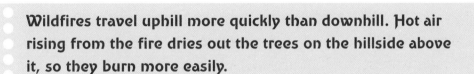

Wildfires travel uphill more quickly than downhill. Hot air rising from the fire dries out the trees on the hillside above it, so they burn more easily.

In 1461 there appeared to be three suns lined up in the sky over Herefordshire, England. The effect was produced by *sundogs* – tiny ice crystals in the sky, which reflect light to make ghostly images of the sun.

A potato is no more fattening than an apple – they have about the same number of calories. It's how the potato is cooked (often with oil or butter) that can make it fattening.

In March 1911, snow that was 11.46 metres (37 feet 7 inches) deep fell in California, USA.

Meghalaya in India has 1,187 millimetres (467 inches) of rain a year, making it the rainiest place in the world.

The roots of some pine trees can extend for 48 kilometres (over 30 miles).

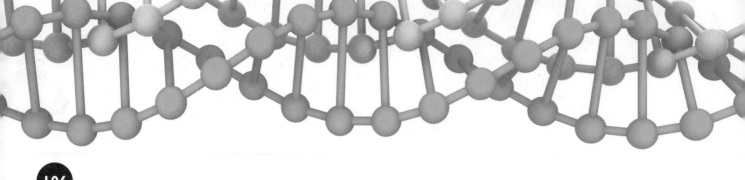

Cyanide is a poison that can be made from several plants. A tiny amount is deadly in just five minutes.

The smallest type of tree is a *dwarf willow* that grows in Greenland. It is only 5 centimetres (2 inches) tall.

Some plants, including grass, produce a poison when something starts to eat them. This is a chemical response to protect the rest of the plant.

A *puffball fungus* can release 7 billion spores in a single day. Luckily, they don't all grow, or there would be fungi everywhere you looked!

Many animals including foxes, squirrels, cockroaches and mice have adapted to urban living. Cities aren't their natural habitat, but there's lots of food and it's nice and warm – why would they ever leave?!

Some fungi glow in the dark and can be seen from 15 metres (50 feet) away. They are used as natural lanterns.

A book of plants published in England in 1597 claimed that tomatoes are poisonous. The author acknowledged that they were eaten regularly in Spain and Italy, though!

If a chicken is caught up in a tornado, its feathers can be ripped out – but it can still survive.

The taste of rat poison varies in different countries. It is adapted to suit the food rats are most used to.

The seeds of the orchid flower are so light that just over 1 million of them weigh only one gram (0.035 ounces).

Some plants grow faster if they are played music. Researchers found the most effective music was 'Bat out of Hell' by the singer Meatloaf!

Some desert plants have adapted to their dry environment by growing really long roots that suck water from deep underground.

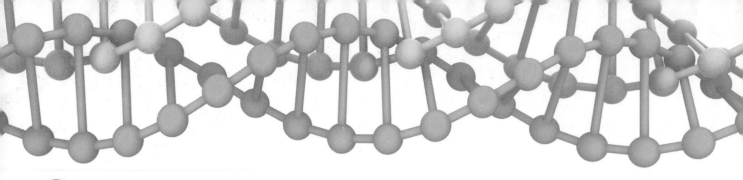

Fungus isn't only mushrooms and toadstools. Mould growing on food that's gone bad is fungus, and so are some nasty things that can grow on your body – like mould on your feet.

The air around a bolt of lightning is five times as hot as the surface of the sun.

The present rate of extinction may be 140,000 species a year.

Minus 40 degrees Celsius is the same temperature as minus 40 degrees Fahrenheit.

The largest living thing on earth is a giant fungus that covers 10 square kilometres (3.86 square miles) in Oregon, USA. It is thought to be around 2,400 years old, but may even be as old as 8,650 years.

The *saguaro cactus* can live for up to 200 years and grow to 18 metres (59 feet) tall. It stores up to 8 tonnes (17.637 pounds) of water inside it – but don't cut one open for a drink in the desert as it's poisonous to humans!

Only 0.001 per cent of the earth's water is in clouds or falling rain at any one time.

If you put a flower in water containing ink, you can turn it blue or black!

Getting parasites is a pain, but getting *parasitoids* means certain death – they live on or inside you, gradually eating you! But they mostly occur only in insects, so you don't need to worry (unless you're an insect).

Plastic trees are being planted in the desert of Saudi Arabia to combat climate change! The idea is that water will condense in them at night, and slowly evaporate during the day, gradually cooling the climate. Clever trick!

Recycling 1 tonne (2,205 pounds) of paper saves 17 trees from being cut down.

A raindrop falls at 11 kilometres (7 miles) per hour.

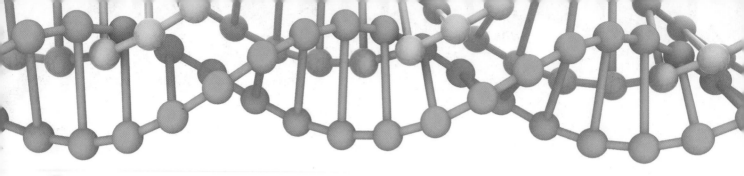

A lightning bolt is around 7.6 centimetres (3 inches) wide and 2 miles (3.2 kilometres) long.

Scientists working in the rainforests often find their feet go green and mouldy. The fungus, which usually breaks down old leaves on the forest floor, is just as happy living on a wet, smelly foot.

Lightning kills about 2,000 people every year.

A patch of rainforest the size of a football pitch can be home to 200 different kinds of tree.

The expression 'once in a blue moon' means that something hardly ever happens. A blue moon does happen occasionally, though – It happened in 1950 when a large wildfire in Canada sent soot high up into the sky making the moon look blue.

A peanut is not really a nut – it grows underground!

There is not always thunder with lightning.

The South American *stinkhorn fungus* smells of rotten meat and old toilets and has a slimy white spike which is irresistible to flies. Not a good pot-plant for your bedroom!

Genetic engineering can combine genes from different plants and animals. A gene from a deep sea fish can be added to a vegetable to make it frost resistant! Some people call *genetically modified* foods like this 'Frankenstein foods'.

The *walking or stilt palm* walks to a better spot if it doesn't like where it's living! The tree grows up to 70 feet tall in the Amazon. Stilts hold it up and support its central trunk. To move, the tree grows more stilts on one side, and then lets the other ones die so that it slowly moves along.

Avalanches can reach speeds of 130 kilometres (80 miles) an hour within 5 seconds of their initial movement.

Some cold-water coral reefs have been growing since the end of the last ice age – 10,000 years ago.

Some trees can live for a very long time. A *redwood tree* which fell over in California, USA, in 1977 is thought to have been 6,200 years old – which means it started to grow 2,000 years before the earliest human civilizations started.

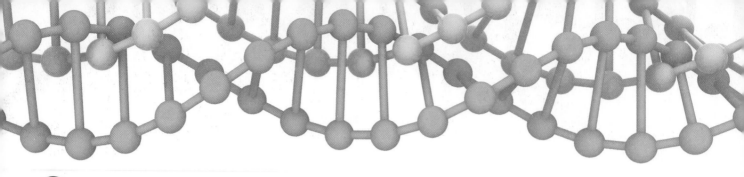

Seeds from the *lotus plant* can grow after lying around for 3,000 years. That's a long lie-in!

The *durian fruit* smells foul – like rotting fish – but tastes great! It's a favourite of orang-utans.

A *tromatolite* is a blob of algae and mud found on Australian beaches, naturally sculpted into the shape of a mushroom.

Instead of guard dogs, *trumpet trees* have 'guard ants' living in their trunks! In return for their home, the *Azteca ants* bite anything that nibbles on the tree and then squirt acid into the creature's wound to make it extra sore. Ouch!

The main source of food for animals that live in the deep sea is *marine snow* – flakes of dead things and faeces from creatures who livehigher up in the water!

There are 1,500 types of insect in one rainforest tree in the Amazon, including 50 types of ant!

In 1982, Japanese
scientists found a
10,000-year-old magnolia
seed in a storage pit.
They managed to grow
it into a tree!

The *strychnine plant* has fruit that
looks like tiny oranges – but don't
be tempted to eat them as
strychnine is a deadly poison.
The tiniest amount can kill you!

A field of *fescue grass*, which
grows in Canada, looks like lots of
little plants, but is really a single
plant that's hundreds of years old.

Algae can live almost anywhere – they get into rocks
through tiny cracks which leave them just enough
sunlight to keep them alive.

The coldest place on earth is Vostok in
Antarctica, where the temperature falls to nearly
minus 90 degrees Celsius (minus 129 degrees
Fahrenheit). Unsurprisingly, no one lives there!

In 2001 a geologist in India found
fossilized raindrops! The imprint was
found in ancient rocks, proving that it
rained on earth 1.6 billion years ago.

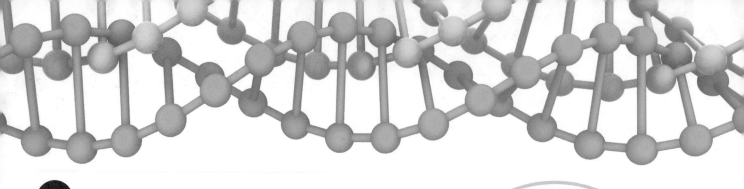

The Australian *bloodwood tree* oozes red sap that looks like blood when it is cut.

The *saguaro cactus* has a woody skeleton inside it! Some animals live in the skeleton once the plant has died.

A pinch of soil holds 5 billion bacteria – nearly enough for everyone on the planet to have one each!

In 1957, passengers aboard *The Edinburgh Castle* sailing down the English Channel saw a row of ships on the horizon – some were upside-down and others were on top of each other. It was a trick of the light caused by hot and cold layers of air reflecting the light strangely!

Window plants in the Namib Desert grow transparent crystals on their leaves to protect them from the hot sun.

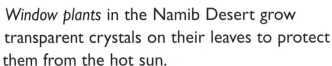

A pumpkin can grow roots with a total length of 24 kilometres (15 miles).

Plants often grow inside the skeletons of dead bodies in the Arctic – they make warm homes and have lots of nutrients that nourish plants.

Some explorers have drunk the juice inside *pitcher plants* – a mixture of the plant's acidic digestive juices and its half-dissolved victims. Yum.

The largest bacteria are 1 millimetre (0.039 inches) long and are big enough to see with the naked eye.

Avalanches kill over 150 people worldwide every year. They are mostly skiers and snowboarders.

Scientists believe 70 per cent of dinosaurs are yet to be discovered, as more new species have been found in the last 20 years than ever before.

The *pink petticoat plant* has a flower that looks like a pretty petticoat – it might look nice but it gobbles up bugs that crawl inside it.

The *anacampseros plant* looks like a bird dropping to protect it from being eaten by animals.

A 'doomsday vault' is being built in an Arctic cave to store seeds from all the world's food-giving plants in case a major disaster wipes them all out. It will contain 4.5 million seed samples that will be able to survive for up to 1,000 years.

All the animals on earth combined use 10,000 tonnes (over 22 million pounds) of oxygen a second.

Ice is technically a mineral.

Over 99 per cent of all the species in the world that have ever lived are already extinct!

The *twin-spurred pitcher plant* is also home to ants that eat some of the insects that fall in. The plant doesn't mind, the ants break up the insects making them easier for the meat-eating plant to digest.

In 90 per cent of avalanche accidents, the snow fall is triggered by a human being.

Brazil nut trees grow happily in the rainforest environment and refuse to grow anywhere else in the world. Scientists have tried to remove them to cultivate in labs, but the trees don't like it.

The frequency of major hurricanes and storms has doubled over the last hundred years, possibly as a result of climate change.

When polar ice melts, it sometimes reveals woolly mammoths frozen since the end of the last ice age. The mammoth meat can still be fresh – on one occasion, dogs ate the defrosted mammoth before scientists could investigate it!

Without starfish, the populations of mussels and sea urchins (which are only eaten by starfish) would explode, destroying the ecosystem of the world's oceans.

Inside the vents of active volcanoes bacteria live in conditions equivalent to a vat of *hydrochloric acid*. They're not fussy about their homes!

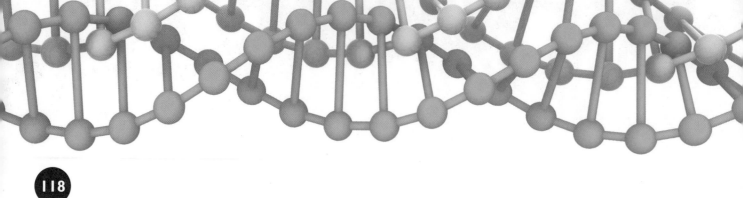

Creosote bushes, which grow in North America, can live for 10,000 years.

The South Pole has no sun for 182 days each year.

The very highest clouds, around 80 kilometres (50 miles) above the earth, are visible after sunset. Scientists think they are made of ice crystals and dust from meteors.

Some seeds eat meat! The seeds of *shepherd's purse* fill with water, swell up and burst – revealing a slimy layer. Bugs that stick to the slime are dissolved as the slimy seed eat them.

If you are trapped in an avalanche, you have a 93 per cent chance of survival if you are rescued within 15 minutes. These odds fall to between 20 and 30 per cent if you are under the snow for 45 minutes. It's very rare for someone to survive longer than two hours.

The word 'hurricane' comes from the name *Huracan* – a Mayan god responsible for storms.

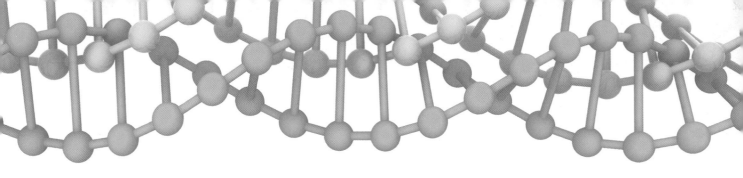

Shocking
Planet Earth Facts

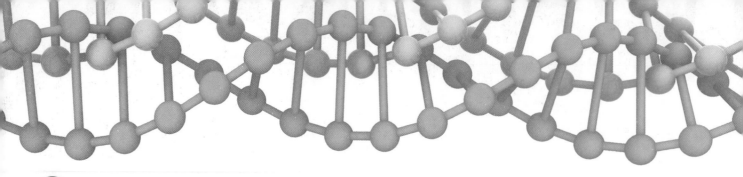

Hawaii has a beach with green sand. It's the only one known, and was produced by *olivine* — a volcanic rock that smashed into tiny grains.

In the last 550 million years, there have been five events that have each destroyed at least 50 per cent of all life on the planet.

For 186 days of the year, the Sun is not visible at the North Pole.

Some rocks float on water. *Pumice stone* is hardened volcanic lava. It often contains so many air bubbles that it is light enough to float.

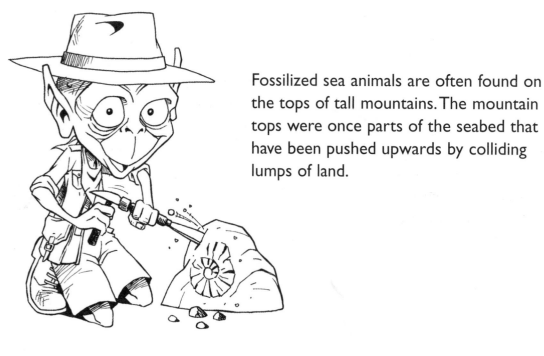

Fossilized sea animals are often found on the tops of tall mountains. The mountain tops were once parts of the seabed that have been pushed upwards by colliding lumps of land.

When lightning strikes a beach, it melts the sand, which hardens again as a type of glass called *fulgurite*. It often forms in twisty tube shapes.

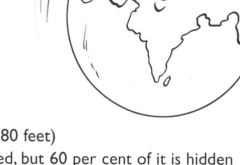

The world's tallest mountain looks quite flat! *Mauna Kea* in Hawaii is 10,205 metres (33,480 feet) tall from its base on the seabed, but 60 per cent of it is hidden under the sea and the rest doesn't look very pointy!

Earth is getting fat! It is gradually getting thicker around the middle, becoming more pumpkin-shaped than round.

Nearly an eighth of the earth's surface is dry desert where less than 25 centimetres (10 inches) of rain falls in a year.

The largest desert in the world also contains most of the world's fresh water! Antarctica qualifies as a desert as it has virtually no rainfall.

Water flows from the Amazon river into the sea with such power that even at a distance of 161 kilometres (100 miles) from the coast, it is possible to scoop up fresh Amazonian water from the sea.

The Dead Sea has amazing healing properties. The water is rich in minerals and helps to relieve skin and joint problems.

Earthquakes can cause landslides and avalanches which can cause serious damage in mountainous places.

On 16 December 1811, the Mississippi river flowed backwards as a result of an earthquake!

A *tsunami* is a massive wave that sweeps over the land and destroys everything in its path. It can be 30 metres (100 feet) high when it strikes the shore.

Llamas are related to camels. A common ancestor roamed from one land to the other when Asia and South America were joined up – now they are separated by the Pacific Ocean.

About one tenth of the earth's surface is covered in ice.

Mount Fuji, the volcano that towers over the Japanese capital Tokyo, last erupted in 1707. The earthquakes and tsunami that followed killed 30,000 people and the rice fields were left barren for 100 years.

The *Vredefort crater* in South Africa was created 2 billion years ago by an asteroid or comet striking Earth. It's big enough to fit 270,000 tennis courts inside!

The *lava* (molten rock) that erupts out of a volcano can be as hot as 1,200 degrees Celsius (2,200 degrees Fahrenheit) and the power of a large eruption can equal that of a million nuclear bombs.

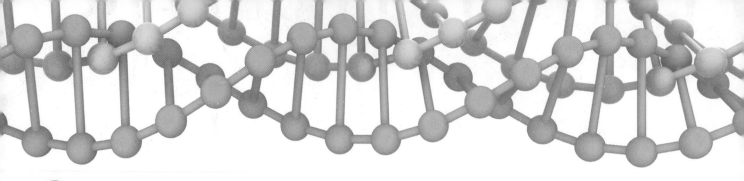

The Antarctic ice sheet contains 90 per cent of all the fresh water on Earth.

Obsidian is a naturally occurring shiny black glass, made when volcanic lava cools very fast. Its edges are razor sharp.

There is a super volcano underneath Yellowstone Park, USA that last erupted 640,000 years ago. If it erupted now, ash would be thrown over the whole of the USA and the entire world's climate would change – perhaps enough to wipe out humans completely.

If you lie in the Dead Sea, you float very easily! The sea is nine times as salty as the Mediterranean – too salty for fish to live in – but great to float in!

Enough energy reaches the Earth from the Sun every second to fulfil all our power needs for a year.

Oil and coal are both made from the dead bodies of animals and plants that lived millions of years ago.

The Grand Canyon, USA, was created up to 14,000 years ago by the force of water rushing over the rock as the ice melted at the end of the last ice age.

Geysers are fountains of hot water, sometimes above boiling point. The water is heated by molten rock under the Earth's crust, and then bubbles back up to the surface under great pressure.

The effects of global warming can be extreme – rising temperatures leading to catastrophic floods and droughts could destroy many plants animals and humans in years to come.

Sound travels through granite rock ten times faster than it travels through air.

The Earth's *crust* – the solid surface of the Earth that holds the land and sea – is extremely thin. If the Earth were an apple, the crust would be about the thickness of the skin.

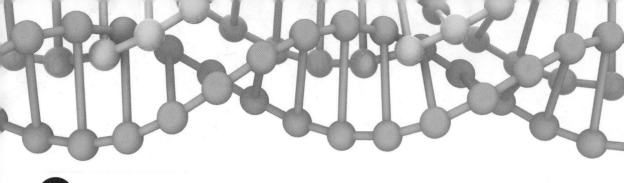

One of the largest volcanic eruptions recorded in recent history occurred on the island of Krakatau in Indonesia in 1883. It was so huge that most of the island disappeared into the sea!

A major eruption of Mount Fuji is long overdue – it usually erupts about once a century...

The temperature at the Earth's centre can reach 7,000 degrees Celsius (12,600 degrees Fahrenheit).

A beach in Hawaii is called *Barking Sands* because the sand seems to 'bark' like a dog when it's walked on. The dry grains make a strange sound when rubbed together.

180 million years ago, India was an island off the coast of Australia. The Earth's land masses slowly move around, at up to 10 centimetres (4 inches) a year.

The largest mountain ranges on Earth are under the sea! They form an area called the *mid-ocean ridge,* which stretches all around the world running through the Pacific, Indian and Atlantic Oceans.

When the volcano Krakatau erupted in Indonesia in 1883, it made the loudest noise in recorded history – it could be heard hundreds of miles away and the sound waves travelled around the globe at least three times!

The gases of the Earth's atmosphere reach up to 700 kilometres (435 miles) high!

Under the sea, rock moves around slowly and is recycled! It goes back under the surface of the Earth to melt and re-emerges through volcanoes. The entire seabed is renewed every 150–200 million years.

Sometimes, a volcano explodes with such force that it blows apart completely. When this happens to an island volcano, the whole island can be destroyed.

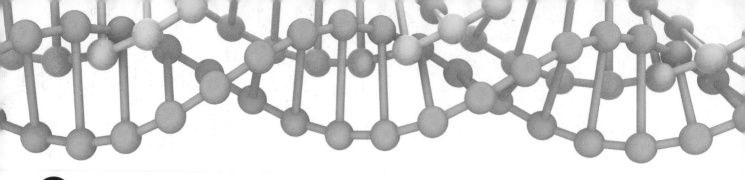

Ice cores are cylinders of ice that scientists have drilled from the polar ice sheets. They give us information about Earth's climate over the last 740,000 years.

The Earth's core is a sphere of metal (mostly iron) about 2,442 kilometres (1,516 miles) across.

Glaciers melting and sea temperatures getting warmer has caused global sea levels to rise between 10 and 25 centimetres (between 4 and 10 inches) in the last century. This is all part of global warming.

The pyramids in Egypt have moved about 4 kilometres (2.5 miles) to the south since they were built around 5,000 years ago because the land masses have shifted.

Lake Nyos in Cameroon, Africa, belches out deadly carbon dioxide. Its poisonous burps killed 1,800 people in one night in August 1986. No one really knows where the gas comes from.

Don Juan Pond in Antarctica is nearly 20 times as salty as the ocean. It's so salty that heavy objects can float on it and it remains a liquid down to temperatures of minus 53 degrees Celsius (minus 63.4 degrees Fahrenheit).

The Atacama desert had no rain at all for more than 400 years, between 1570 and 1971.

Samosir is an island within an island – it is in Lake Toba, on the Indonesian island of Sumatra. The lake formed when the super volcano *Toba* erupted about 70,000 years ago. The island growing in the middle of the lake is actually a new volcano.

The Atacama Desert is so dry that between the years 1964 and 2001, the average rainfall was only 0.5 millimetres (0.01 inches) per year!

A tsunami can travel across the ocean as fast as a jet plane, at speeds of up to 750 kilometres (465 miles) per hour.

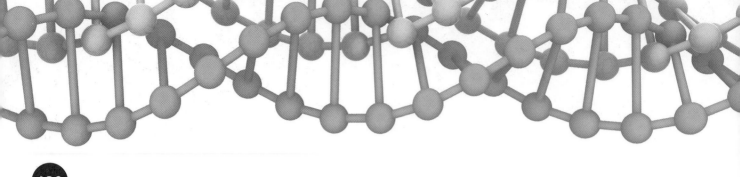

Human storm chasers use special vehicles and equipment to locate and follow storms.

The Pacific Ocean is the largest ocean on Earth. It covers over 155 million square kilometres (60 million square miles) and has an average depth of nearly 4 kilometres (2.5 miles).

Increasing global temperatures could lead to an increase in diseases around the world – they will spread more easily and the weather won't be cold enough to kill them off.

A new island called *Surtur's Island*, near Iceland, was born in 1963! A volcano under the sea poured out lava which hardened and piled up to form the island.

February 1865 is the only month in recorded history to have had no full moon.

The Sargasso Sea is an area in the Atlantic Ocean that is completely still. *Sargassum seaweed* has grown over the surface, stopping the water from moving.

Scorching hot winds from a volcanic eruption can travel at 300 kilometres (185 miles) per hour burning everything in their path at up to 800 degrees Celsius (1,470 degrees Fahrenheit).

Mud avalanches can be deadly as well as messy – they can flow at up to 160 kilometres (100 miles) per hour.

The World Wildlife Fund believes that climate change has wiped out all the golden toads of Costa Rica – making them one of the first victims of global warming.

In some deserts, the sand 'sings'. This eerie sound is produced by the wind moving across the sand.

Pumping water up from under the ground in California is causing the ground there to sink up to 11 centimetres (4 inches) a year!

The *Kilauea* volcano in Hawaii has been erupting constantly since 1983, throwing out 5 cubic metres (176 cubic feet) of lava every second!

One fifth of fresh water that drains into the seas comes from the Amazon river in South America.

When the *Laki* volcano in Iceland erupted in 1783, poisonous gas clouds swamped the land, killing half the country's livestock. A fifth of the human population starved to death.

In 2004, the tsunami in the Indian Ocean killed around 230,000 people and was the ninth deadliest natural disaster since the Middle Ages.

The volcano underneath Yellowstone Park, USA, could erupt at any time...

Small icebergs, fitted with sails, have been steered from the Antarctic to Peru, a distance of 3,862 kilometres (2,400 miles)!

One theory suggests that 75,000 years ago, the eruption of the super volcano Toba destroyed so many human lives that only 1,000 couples were left to reproduce!

The city of La Paz in Bolivia is safe from fires – the city is so high up that there is barely enough oxygen to keep a single flame alight.

The continent of Asia accounts for 30 per cent of the Earth's land but is home to 60 per cent of the world's population.

During the first 2.7 billion years on Earth, only single cells existed. Then slime moulds, sponges and other very simple forms of life evolved. Everything else has appeared in the last billion years.

A lake in Chile mysteriously disappeared in 2007. The glacial lake had water under a crust of ice. But at some point in 2007, the water disappeared completely and only chunks of ice were left behind.

Scientists in Colorado, USA, spent decades trying to help restock rivers with an endangered fish, but they used the wrong one! Many of the fish they released into the rivers were just ordinary fish that looked like the endangered one!

Melting arctic ice has uncovered a previously unknown island, now called *Warming Island*, off the coast of Greenland.

Lake Vostok lies buried under 4 kilometres (2.5 miles) of ice in Antarctica yet is full of liquid water. It was last open to the air around half a million years ago and was discovered by radar in 1994.

You can die of thirst in the desert in only two days. You'd need to drink 9 litres (about 16 pints) of water a day to stay healthy on a desert trek!

Daintree National Park in Australia is famous for its bouncing stones – they can be bounced off each other like balls! It's said that people who steal the stones get cursed…

Mass extinctions of life on Earth appear to happen about every 26 million years. So don't worry just yet!

More people die in floods than in other types of natural disasters. The Yellow River flood in China in 1931 killed between one and four million people, and is the deadliest known natural disaster.

The Sahara desert has an *aridity score* of 200 – that means it loses 200 times the amount of water that it gains!

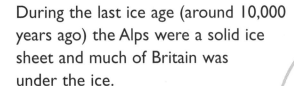

During the last ice age (around 10,000 years ago) the Alps were a solid ice sheet and much of Britain was under the ice.

Bear faeces are an essential part of the North American ecosystem! Grizzly bears eat salmon from the streams and then deposit vital nutrients on the land in the form of droppings and leftover fish.

Some volcanic eruptions produce finely spun strings of glass that look like candyfloss.

According to some scientists, the Sahara desert is moving forward at a rate of 6 kilometres (3.7 miles) a year.

A volcanic eruption destroyed the Roman city of Pompeii in AD79. The energy the eruption released was 100,000 times more powerful than that of the atomic bomb dropped on Hiroshima, Japan, in 1945.

The shores of the Dead Sea in the Middle East are the lowest dry land on Earth, at around 400 metres (1,312 feet) below sea level.

One victim of global warming is the *Ilulissat* glacier in Greenland, which is melting and flowing into the sea more quickly than ever before.

The world's largest hot desert, the Sahara, is almost as big as the USA – it covers 9 million square kilometres (3.5 million square miles).

Of the 3 per cent fresh water in the world, two thirds exists as ice – only 1 per cent of Earth's water is fresh and in liquid form.

An *iron–manganese* crust grows on rocks under the sea. This thickens the Earth's crust – but only by about 1 millimetre (0.04 inches) every million years.

The Earth's inner core spins more quickly than the outside. Every 400 years, the inner core makes one complete extra revolution compared to the outside. (Not all in one go – it's just going a bit quicker for the whole 400 years!)

If the entire Antarctic ice sheet were to melt, sea levels would rise by 67 metres (220 feet), leaving cities such as New York, Hong Kong and London completely lost under the water.

Mount *Cotopaxi* in Ecuador is on the equator, usually the hottest area on earth – but it has a glacier! The mountain is so high that the glacier stays frozen.

Tornado Alley is an area in the USA from central Texas to the border of Canada that has the perfect weather conditions for tornadoes.

The oldest rocks in the world are four billion years old.

One tenth of the Earth's surface is permanently under ice and 90 per cent of that ice is found in Antarctica.

Areas of Sweden and Finland are still rising as a result of the ice from last ice age melting. The land raises about 1 metre (3.28 feet) in 100 years.

More than 99 per cent of Antarctica is covered in snow and ice.

Earthquakes can cause fires when the damage they do breaks electrical or gas lines.

Escape velocity – the speed you need to travel to escape Earth's gravity is 11.2 kilometres (6.95 miles) per second.

One method of stopping a wildfire is to start another one! By burning an area ahead of the fire, it's possible to remove the fuel the wildfire needs to keep going.

San Francisco and Los Angeles, USA, are moving towards each other at the rate of 5 centimetres (2 inches) a year. They are due to collide in about 15 million years.

The Richter scale measures the size of an earthquake and goes from 1 (small) to 10 (deadly). The largest earthquake ever recorded was a 9.5 in Chile, in 1960. An earthquake measuring 12 would break the Earth in half!

There are more volcanoes in the mid-ocean ridge than there are on land.

A tsunami occurred in Alaska in 1958 that was 524 metres (1,719 feet) tall – even taller than the Empire State Building.

Antarctica is the only continent with no native people. Around 4,000 scientists live there in the Antarctic summer, and 1,000 in the winter, making it the least densely populated land on Earth.

The Arctic may be totally free of ice for 3 months each year by 2040 due to global warming.

450 million years ago, the South Pole was located where the Sahara Desert is now.

There are around 10 billion tonnes (22 thousand pounds) of gold in the oceans, but it is too difficult to extract it!

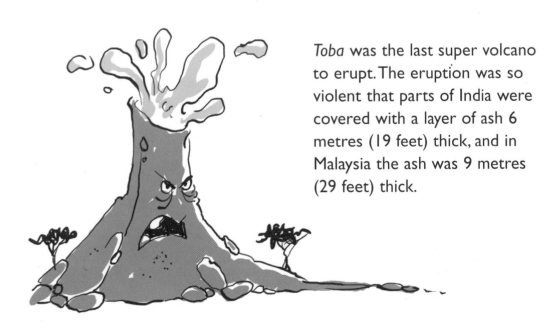

Toba was the last super volcano to erupt. The eruption was so violent that parts of India were covered with a layer of ash 6 metres (19 feet) thick, and in Malaysia the ash was 9 metres (29 feet) thick.

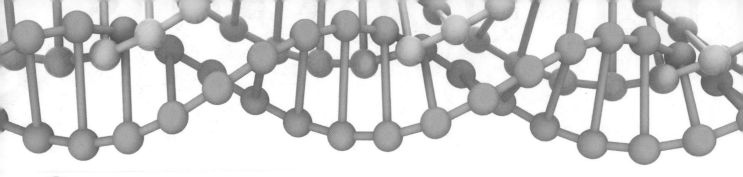

Polar bears could be extinct in 100 years if climate change continues to melt the ice at the North Pole.

Some people think the legendary lost city of Atlantis was on a volcanic island that exploded, destroying the city.

Hydrothermal vents spit scalding-hot steam that is heated underground. Water around one hydrothermal vent near the west coast of the USA can reach 400 degrees Celsius (752 degrees Fahrenheit).

There are 8,000 small earthquakes (measuring less than 2 on the Richter scale) each day – they are too small for people to even feel them.

Only 3 per cent of the water on Earth is fresh water – the other 97 per cent is salt water in the seas.

Shocking Space Facts

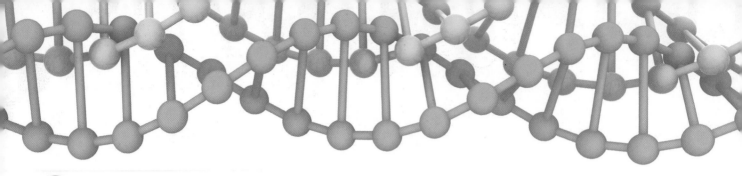

Some astronauts have suffered from an illness called *lunar lung* caused by breathing in moon dust.

The surface of the planet Venus has an average temperature of 480 degrees Celsius (896 degrees Fahrenheit). it's unlikely to be the first planet humans visit, unless they want a tan…

There are hundreds of billions of galaxies in the universe… too many to count, in fact!

Saturn is the least dense planet – it would float on water!

A *black hole* is an area in space with a gravitational field that is so strong, that nothing inside it can ever escape – not even light – which is how they got their rather dark name…

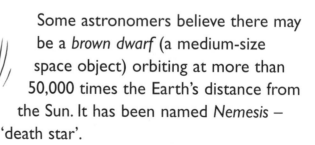

Some astronomers believe there may be a *brown dwarf* (a medium-size space object) orbiting at more than 50,000 times the Earth's distance from the Sun. It has been named *Nemesis* – 'death star'.

Astronauts wear nappies during take off, landing and on space walks, as they can't go to the lavatory at these times!

Comets and asteroids are made from the bits and pieces left over from the creation of the Solar System. If someone had tidied up properly, there wouldn't be any!

Early space travellers weren't equipped with hot water to rehydrate food, so they ate small, dry cubes of food or meals they squeezed out of tubes.

It is thought that the Moon was formed when a planet collided with Earth and knocked off a huge chunk, about 4.5 billion years ago.

An early warning system designed to tell us if an asteroid is about to hit the Earth mistook the *Rosetta* spacecraft for a rock that had got dangerously close!

Space lavatories have straps for the astronauts' feet and thighs to stop them from drifting off the lavatory halfway through!

Asteroids are small, rocky astronomical objects that orbit the Sun. Hundreds of thousands have been discovered and they can sometimes behave like planets.

The Sun accounts for 98 per cent of the mass of the Solar System.

The Crab Nebula is an area of really bright gas and was formed by an exploding star. The explosion was seen by Chinese astronomers in 1054 and was bright enough to be seen with the naked eye in daylight for 23 days after that.

A *white dwarf* is the leftover centre of a star that has used up all its nuclear fuel. As they get older, they keep on getting cooler, and can crystallize to form gigantic diamonds!

NASA – the National Aeronautics and Space Administration founded in the USA in 1958 – has developed ways to collect sweat from exercising astronauts to convert into drinking water for them in space. They can also do this with urine!

The Solar System is the collection of 9 planets that orbit the Sun with their moons and other matter. It didn't form until nearly 10 billion years after the start of the universe.

Mars' moons are shaped like potatoes!

The most distant black hole known to man is 13 billion light years away. It weighs 3 billion times as much as the Sun.

Russian cosmonaut, Sergei Avdeyev, holds the current record for time travel by a human being. He has spent so long orbiting the Earth at 27,000 kilometres (17,000 miles) per hour that he has travelled 0.02 seconds into the future!

The debris from the *Crab Nebula* explosion is still travelling through the universe at 1,800 kilometres (1,100 miles) per second.

In 2007, scientists used the internet to link-up telescopes based in China, Europe and Australia to create a single telescope spanning half the Earth.

The temperature of the Sun is 6,000 degrees Celsius (10,832 degrees Fahrenheit) on the surface and a scorching 15,000,000 degrees Celsius (27,000,000 degrees Fahrenheit) at the centre.

No one has ever been hit and killed by a falling meteorite, as far as we know...

The atmospheric pressure at the centre of the Sun is 340 billion times greater than at sea level on Earth.

In 2004, astronomers discovered a white dwarf that had turned into a huge diamond! It measures 4,000 kilometres (2,500 miles) across and if it were sold as jewellery it would have 10 billion, trillion, trillion carats!

A spacecraft powered by *photons* (light particles) would build up to a speed of 160,934 kilometres (100,000 miles) per hour after three years.

The Sun loses 1 billion kilograms (2.2 billion pounds) of weight each second.

It takes about 8 minutes for light from the Sun to reach the Earth. So if the Sun went out now, we wouldn't know for 8 minutes!

To get up to speed without using fuel, spacecrafts often use the gravity of planets as a sort of slingshot – the spaceship whizzes around the planet and is thrown out into space. It's called a 'gravity-assist' move.

Pele, the largest volcano on Jupiter's moon, *Io*, erupts to heights 30 times that of Mount Everest. Gas and the other products of the eruption fall over an area the size of France.

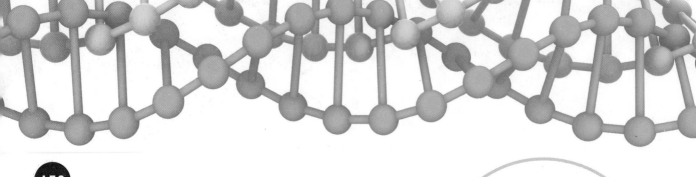

The spaceship Voyager travels at over 56,000 kilometres (35,000 miles) per hour, but even at this speed it will take nearly 40,000 years to reach the very edge of the Solar System.

Some rocks that you find on Earth are in fact pieces of the planet Mars that have fallen from the sky!

Our closest neighbouring star, *Proxima Centauri* is 40 trillion kilometres (25 trillion miles) from Earth. This is 4.24 light years.

NASA's *Pioneer* spacecraft was launched in 1972 on its voyage towards the star *Aldebaran*, but will take two million years to arrive! Its last contact with Earth was in 2003.

The Roman Catholic Church banned the Italian astronomer, Galileo Galilei (1564–1642), from teaching that the Earth travels around the Sun. They did not withdraw their objection until 1992, by which time he wasn't too bothered…

The Russian spacecraft, *Venera 1*, was ahead of its time. It flew to the planet Venus in 1961 – seven years before *Apollo 7* orbited the Moon.

It took a total of 11,000 accumulated years of work and preparation to send the Voyager spacecraft to Neptune.

In 1974, the *Arecibo* telescope on Puerto Rico sent out a coded message towards the *M13 cluster* of 300,000 stars. It is 21,000 light years away from Earth, so if anything living there replies to the message, we will not receive the answer for 42,000 years!

In space, yoghurt will still stay on a spoon, where other foods will float off and drift around the space ship.

The best planet to live on to get most birthdays is Mercury. A year lasts only 88 days, so when you're 10 on Earth you'd be 41 and a half on Mercury! But don't worry – instead of living to around 80 years old, you'd live to be 332!

If you travelled into a black hole, your body would be 'spaghettified' – drawn out into an incredibly long, thin strand. Best not try!

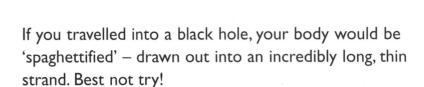

Enceladus, a moon of the planet Saturn, has ice volcanoes that erupt water.

The *Voyager* spacecrafts carry gold-plated disks containing images and sounds from Earth. They include spoken greetings in 55 languages, including an ancient language not spoken for 6,000 years. They also contain whale music and other animal sounds – so any aliens listening to it might think that humans all talk in 'whale'!

Most of the mass of the universe (96 per cent) is made up of mysterious 'dark matter' that we can't see at all and know nothing about...

The International Space Station is a $100 billion (about £51 billion) laboratory orbiting the Earth. It has been under construction since 1998, and should be completed in 2010.

The star *Alpha Herculis* is 25 times larger than the diameter of the Earth's orbit around the Sun.

The science of modelling planets so that human life can live on them is called *terraforming* ('earth shaping'). Tools have been developed for it, even though we haven't found a planet to terraform yet!

Air in the Space Shuttle lavatories is cleaned to remove smells and bacteria before it is pumped back into the living area.

In 1957, a stray dog called Laika became the first dog in space. She went on the satellite *Sputnik* 2 launched by the USSR, but died in space because the satellite had no means of returning to Earth.

The Solar System travels at 273 kilometres (170 miles) per second around the centre of our galaxy, the Milky Way.

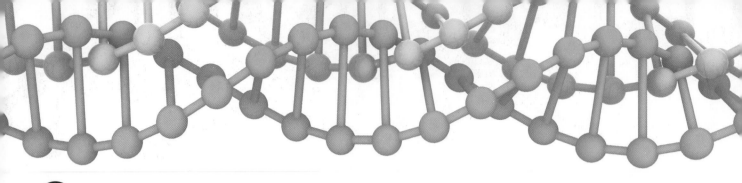

The stars of the Milky Way revolve around its centre, completing one orbit every 200–250 million years.

Some scientists think that a large asteroid exploded over the North America 12,900 years ago, wiping out Stone Age human life and many other animals. The blast caused a nuclear winter – blotting out the Sun creating low temperatures that also affected Europe and Asia.

Some scientists claim they have discovered 'rogue planets' which do not orbit any star but wander through space on their own.

Around 40,000 tonnes (88 million pounds) of meteoric dust hits Earth each year.

The magnetic poles of the Sun switch places every eleven years in a cycle called *Solarmax*. The Earth's magnetic poles do this too, but much less regularly.

When the Moon is directly overhead, you weigh slightly less than at all other times, because of the effect of its gravity.

Earth travels 2.4 million kilometres (1.5 million miles) a day around the Sun.

The 'Vomit Comet' is the name given to an aircraft that flies in such a way that it produces weightlessness. It's used to train astronauts, carry out research and even make movies. It tends to make people sick, as you could probably guess…

It takes 1.25 seconds for light, reflected by the Moon to reach Earth.

The effects of zero gravity on the human body are so severe that astronauts who stay in space for a long time suffer muscle wasting and loss of bone density. They can be unwell for months or sometimes years after their return to Earth.

The size of the universe is so vast compared to the matter it contains that it's equivalent to a box, measuring 32 kilometres (20 miles) in all dimensions, containing one grain of sand.

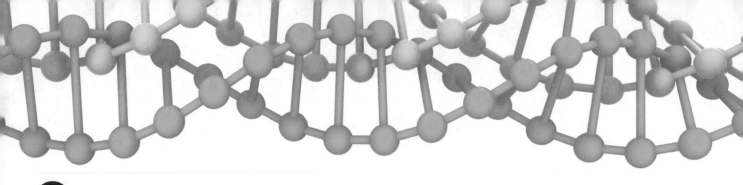

The temperature on the Moon can change 380 degrees Celsius (500 degrees Fahrenheit) from day to night, as there is no atmosphere there to trap the heat of the Sun.

On Jupiter, a day is just under 10 'Earth hours' long.

Aliens on distant planets could pick up human radio broadcasts from 80 years ago. Radio travels at the speed of light, so broadcasts from 80 years ago will now be reaching planets 80 light years from Earth. If aliens living on planets only 40 light years away have sent a reply, it will arrive any day now!

By October 2007, scientists had discovered 263 *exoplanets* – planets that are not in our own Solar System. Most are gas giants, like Jupiter.

The International Space Station can be seen orbiting the Earth with the naked eye! The best time to look for it is after sunset.

Could there be aliens in Italy? Investigators in Sicily, who were unable to find the cause of domestic appliances suddenly bursting into flames in 2004, suggested that aliens might be testing secret weapons...

Jupiter is twice as big as all the other planets in the Solar System combined.

Atomic clocks run more accurately in space where they are not affected by gravity.

Black holes can 'sing'. A black hole in the *Perseus* galaxy, 300 million light years away, has been emitting an extremely low musical sound for two billion years. X-rays can detect it, but we can't hear it.

If you could drive an ordinary car to the Sun, travelling at 80 kilometres (50 miles) per hour it would take over 212 years to get there!

There is a planet similar to Earth, with ideal conditions for human life. It's 20.5 light years from Earth so if we sent a message to the planet, it would be 41 years before we got a reply.

Astronomers have found a planet outside our Solar System that has water. Unfortunately, it's a gas giant with a temperature of 1,100 degrees Celsius (212 degrees Fahrenheit), and all the water exists as vapour. It's also 150 million light years away, but its existence means there's likely to be other water-bearing planets out there.

On the International Space Station, all waste from the lavatories is stored in a supply craft called *The Progress*. The craft is eventually released and burns away in Earth's atmosphere.

NASA intends to build a 'town' on the Moon before the year 2030.

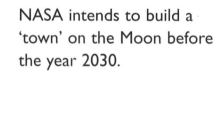

The coldest temperature possible is called absolute zero. It is minus 273.15 degrees Celsius (minus 459.67 degrees Fahrenheit) and is the temperature at which atoms and molecules stop moving.

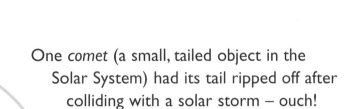

One *comet* (a small, tailed object in the Solar System) had its tail ripped off after colliding with a solar storm – ouch!

Wormholes (if they exist) are tunnels through space and time, which could possibly be used for time travel.

A radio signal from space known as the 'Wow!' signal, has never been explained and could be real evidence of intelligent life. It was picked up in 1977 and has never been repeated.

Solid waste from space lavatories on shuttles is compressed and stored for return to Earth; liquid waste is thrown out into space.

An astronaut standing on one of Mars' moons would see Mars as a vast red orb – 80 times larger than a full moon looks to us.

The International Space Station is equipped with huge solar panels and all its power comes from the Sun.

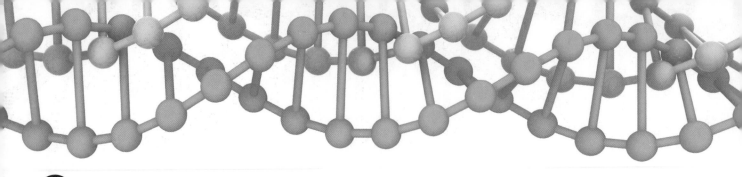

Our Solar System is a youngster in the big happy family of the universe – it's only 4.5 billion years old. The oldest stars are around 13 billion years old.

Time goes more slowly near things that exert a lot of gravitational force, such as large stars.

The Sun is not the largest thing in the Solar System – the comet *Holmes* is even bigger. Although the solid centre of the comet is only 3.6 kilometres (2.2 miles) across, the *coma* (the cloud of dust and gas around it) is wider than the Sun.

New research suggests that Earth's moon is around 30 million years younger than was previously thought!

The Kuiper Belt is a band of leftover debris from the formation of the planets, and circles the Sun beyond the orbit of Neptune. It contains at least 70,000 objects that measure more than 100 kilometres (62 miles) across.

Jupiter leaves a huge trail of gas as it moves around the Sun. Like the tail of a comet, it streams out 650 million kilometres (400 million miles) behind the planet.

Astronauts use special shampoo that they don't have to wash out of their hair.

The Oort Cloud is a vast cloud of comets on the very edge of the Solar System. It houses trillions of comets that measure over 1.3 kilometres (0.8 miles) across.

The outer band of the Oort Cloud may be 30,000 times the distance of the Earth from the Sun, from one edge to the other. Although it contains trillions of lumps of rock, it is probably only a few times the mass of the Earth.

Scientists think *wormholes* (tunnels through space and time) may be so tiny that they are narrower than a single atom.

If we could hollow out Saturn, 764 Earths would fit inside it!

The largest known comet tail is 500 million kilometres (310 million miles) long and belongs to *Comet Hyakutake.*

Mercury's day is so long, you'd only get breakfast once every two years! It takes the planet nearly two Earth years to revolve once, so a day takes a whole year and so does a night!

The Moon is moving away from the Earth at a rate of about 4 centimetres (1.6 inches) a year.

A year on *Sedna*, the *planetoid* (an asteroid with characteristics of a planet), lasts 10,500 Earth years. It's been the same year there since the end of the last Ice Age on Earth!

There is a plan to send a robotic mission to Mars to fetch some of the planet's soil within the next 10 years.

Neptune can't be seen with the naked eye. It was the first planet to have been predicted by mathematical observations rather than actually spotted.

If we could hollow out Saturn, 764 Earths would fit inside it!

If you weigh 45 kilograms (100 pounds) on Earth, you would weigh only 17 kilograms (38 pounds) on Mars because of the difference in gravity. No need for diets on Mars then!

There are no seasons on Jupiter. The planet does not tilt enough on its axis to produce temperature differences during the year.

Some scientists think there may be a zone in the atmosphere of Venus, about 50 kilometres (31 miles) above the surface, where life could exist. Don't think in terms of humans or animals, though – they're only expecting to find tiny micro-organisms.

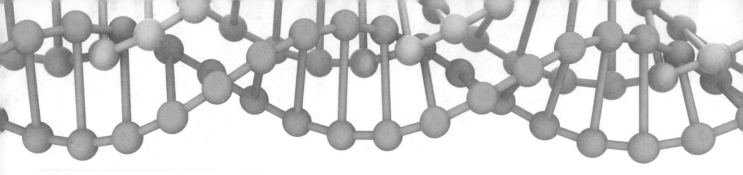

In 2007 a comet called _17/P Holmes_ got 1 million times brighter in 36 hours!

If you managed to fall right into a black hole and stay conscious you may carry on falling forever – time effectively stands still, so you'd never get to the bottom!

A hurricane on Jupiter has lasted for at least 300 years. That was when people invented telescopes enabling them to see it – but it could have been there before that. The storm is twice the size of Earth!

Each astronaut has their own personal urine funnel, which they attach to the space station toilet.

A day on Neptune takes only 19 Earth hours, but a Neptune year is 165 Earth years long – so there are around 75,000 days in a year on Neptune.

The temperature on dwarf planet Pluto is thought to be between minus 240 and minus 210 degrees Celsius (minus 400 to minus 346 Fahrenheit). Wrap up warm if you ever visit!

In conditions of zero gravity, all the blood collects at the top of the body.

In around a billion years, the Sun will have grown so much that the Earth will be too hot to live on. It will, however, make Pluto pleasantly warm and habitable for a while, before the Sun increases in size even more and eventually dies.

NASA uses part of the Arizona desert, USA, to train astronauts. The heat and dust storms make it unpleasant, but the harsh environment is ideal for trying out new equipment and techniques.

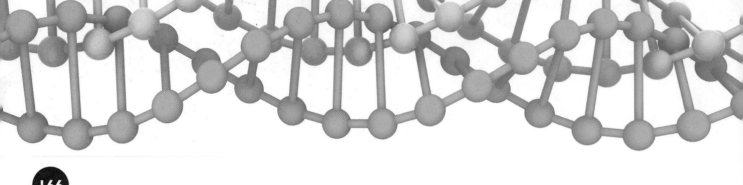

Scientists believe they have found a 'hole' in the universe that may be evidence that another universe exists.

There are 100 billion stars in a typical galaxy.

On NASA's website you can listen to radio broadcasts from Jupiter. There's no music – just the sound of the planet's weather!

To avoid Earth being toasted as the Sun grows, we could move it out towards Pluto. By harnessing energy from a comet, we could gradually move Earth outwards, away from the Sun. Some scientists believe we could have moved the Earth 80 million kilometres (50 million miles) in a few billion years' time.

Astronauts have to spend time in quarantine before and after they go into space.

In space, all liquids (including urine) simultaneously boil and freeze. A liquid that is spilled or dumped into outer space instantly spreads out into a vapour then the droplets freeze into a fine haze of ice crystals.

In two weeks, the Sun produces as much energy as that stored in all the coal, gas and petrol reserves that there have ever been on Earth!

A light year is the distance that light can travel in one year. It works out at about 10 million kilometres (6 million million miles)!

If you managed to get within 161 kilometres (100 miles) of a black hole, you'd be heated up to over 2,000,000 degrees Celsius (3,600,000 degrees Fahrenheit)!

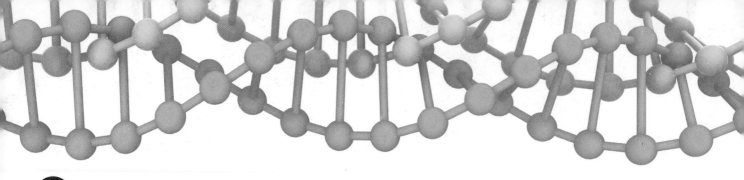

One hundred and three million Earths would fit inside the Sun!

The tallest volcano in the solar system is called *Olympus Mons*. It's peak is 27 kilometres (16.88 miles) above the surface of Mars.

Every atom in your body was once part of a star.

The Earth's core is about the same size as the Moon.

The last time a human stepped on the Moon was in December 1972.

A huge cloud of gas in the middle of our galaxy is made of gaseous alcohol. A piece of the cloud the same volume as the Earth would be needed to produce the equivalent of one just glass of wine!

Shocking
Technology Facts

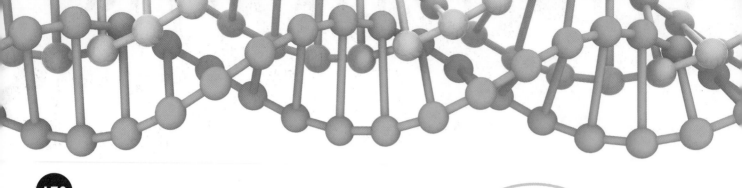

Rubber bands last longer if they are kept in a refrigerator.

Electric bug-zappers actually attract bugs. They only kill a small proportion of the bugs they attract, so you may be bitten by more bugs if you have one than if you don't!

An average-sized teacup can hold around 1 million grains of sand.

There is enough lead in a pencil to draw a line that is 56 kilometres (35 miles) long. You'd need a good pencil sharpener though!

Marek Turowski (UK) reached a speed of 148 kilometres (92 miles) per hour driving a motorized couch in May 2007.

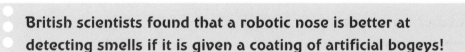

British scientists found that a robotic nose is better at detecting smells if it is given a coating of artificial bogeys!

Scientists are working on a 'cloak of invisibility' that will hide objects by making light waves flow around them, like water flowing around a rock in a river.

There's a reason why tomato ketchup won't come out of the bottle and then falls out in a huge dollop – it's called *shear thinning*. Some thick liquids go thin when shaken but no one knows exactly how it works and scientists can't predict when it will happen.

Amazonian Indians heat *poison arrow frogs* over a fire to sweat the poison out of them. They use the poison to tip their hunting arrows.

Earthrace is said to be the world's fastest eco-boat. It's partly powered by human fat from its crewmembers!

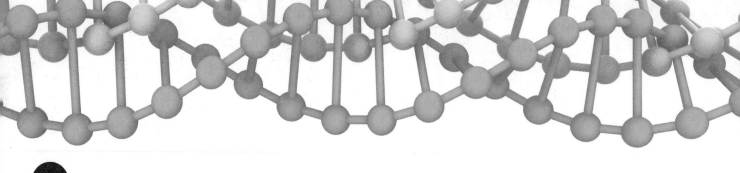

A laser is a very narrow beam of powerful light. It is so straight that it doesn't spread out even over huge distances. A laser beam can be reflected off a mirror on the Moon and return back to Earth in a straight line.

By adding vinegar to red cabbage when you cook it you can make it go pink. Add some bicarbonate of soda to make it turn blue instead.

'Frozen smoke' is a solid that is 99 per cent air – its real name is *aerogel*. It looks transparent but hazy – just like frozen smoke!

The *dandyhorse* was an early form of bicycle in the 1930s. It had no pedals, and you had to push it along by foot.

Recycling one plastic bottle saves enough energy to power a 60-watt light bulb for 3 hours.

Robotarium X in Portugal is the first zoo full of robots, where 45 robots share a steel and glass cage. Some are nice, and respond to visitors. Others are nasty and bite the tails off their companions. How bizarre!

The world's largest working mobile phone is called the Maxi Handy and is 2.05 metres (6.72 feet) tall! It has a colour screen and can send and receive text messages.

When a gas pipeline leaks in the California desert, workers put a chemical into the gas that attracts vultures. The vultures gather where the gas leaks out, so workers only need to spot the vultures to find the leak.

There is no benefit in using striped toothpaste – the stripes are purely to make the toothpaste look more interesting.

Dropping, heating or hammering a magnet can reduce its magnetic power.

A robotic suit is sometimes used to help people recover from nerve damage and learn to move their muscles again.

A boat that scoots over the waves, and looks like a giant spider, was launched in 2007. It can travel 8,000 kilometres (5,000 miles) on one tank of diesel fuel.

It's impossible to fold a dry piece of paper in half more than seven times.

The National Institute for Standards and Technology in the USA has made an atomic clock as small as a grain of rice.

Aconite is one of the most deadly poisons known – yet it is used in homeopathic remedies as a medicine!

If you were to stroke a cat 70 million times, you would generate enough static electricity to power a 60-watt light bulb for one minute. Don't try this one at home…the poor cat would have no hair left!

Liquid helium will crawl up the sides of its container if the top is warmer than the bottom.

In 2001 a robot controlled by surgeons in New York successfully removed the gall bladder from a patient in France.

If a glass of water were magnified to the size of the whole earth, each molecule would be the size of a tennis ball.

Juan Jimenez in Puerto Rico, USA, owns the smallest jet aircraft. It measures 3.7 metres (12 feet) in length, weighs 162 kilograms (358 pounds) and can travel at speeds of 483 kilometres (300 miles) per hour!

An early model of a hovercraft was made from an empty cat food tin, a vacuum cleaner and a coffee tin!

Reports of ghosts have dropped considerably as the use of mobile phones has increased. It seems that the spooks don't like the radio waves!

Scientists are testing the use of blue lights to help keep night drivers awake. They work by convincing the human body clock that it's morning!

Golf balls can sometimes reach speeds of 273 kilometres (170 miles) per hour.

Percy Spencer (USA) invented the microwave oven in 1945, using new technology developed for military defence during the Second World War.

A FogScreen is a curtain of fog, or water vapour, onto which you can project images from a computer or video. Using a FogScreen it's possible to show a film anywhere.

If you whirl a bucket of water around fast enough, the water will not fall out even when the bucket is upside down! This is caused because the *centrifugal force* (that pushes objects outwards) is greater than the force of gravity, which would normally cause the water to fall.

If an electric current is applied to two glasses of water standing next to each other, with the positive electrode in one glass and the negative in the other, the water will climb up the walls of the glass and form a bridge between the two glasses in mid-air to allow the current to flow.

Radar was first used to detect enemy aircraft during the Second World War.

The longest journey ever made on a tractor was 21,199 kilometres (13,172 miles) in Russia in 2005.

Doctors in ancient Egypt would give patients an electric shock with a catfish to treat the pain caused by arthritis.

Many types of toothpaste contain the skeletons of microscopic creatures from the sea, called *diatoms*.

Robotic jaws have been designed which will mimic the action of human ones.

The gas used for cookers and fires has no smell. The gas supply company adds the strong smell deliberately so that people can tell immediately if there is a leak.

Antifreeze is deadly poisonous – some governments insist that manufacturers add a chemical to make it taste horrible to stop people and animals from drinking it.

The world's smallest cinema was built in 1934 and used to use bed sheets as a screen! The *Cinema Dei Piccoli* in Rome, Italy was restored in 1991 and has 63 seats, air conditioning and stereo sound. The bed sheets have been upgraded too!

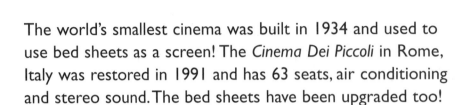

Black light bulbs emit light in the ultraviolet range of the spectrum.

Glow sticks are the only safe form of lighting to use straight after an earthquake. They produce light from the reaction of chemicals sealed inside the stick.

Irons have been used for centuries and used to be heated up in the oven! The first electric ones appeared in 1891.

Wearing an asbestos suit lined with reflective foil, a fire fighter can survive temperatures of 1,093 degrees Celsius (2,000 degrees Fahrenheit).

Salt is the only rock that humans can eat.

It's possible to locate a person using a mobile phone with almost pinpoint accuracy, wherever they are in the world.

The gas inside most light bulbs is not air, but another gas called *argon*.

Human bodies decay more slowly than they used to as food is now packed with preservatives that make their way into the flesh – and preserve us too!

A robotic caterpillar controlled by a joystick can be inserted through a small hole in the chest, and crawl over a person's heart to inject drugs or install implants to heal any damage.

Russian scientists are experimenting with concrete submarines. They would not show up on sonar displays, as they would look the same as rocks or sand.

Bubbles of gas produced by bacteria form the holes in Swiss cheese.

In terms of its size, a laser is a brighter light than the Sun.

An average household's annual waste contains enough unreleased energy to power a television for 5,000 hours.

Pykrete is a rock-hard solid made of frozen water and sawdust. It is ten times tougher than just ordinary ice and melts more slowly.

If you bend a piece of dry spaghetti until it breaks it will always fall into more than two pieces.

Roman engineers were ahead of their time. They heated chalk and seashells at over 900 degrees Celsius (1,650 degrees Fahrenheit) to make lime, to which they added volcanic ash, to make concrete.

Diamonds are made from the same chemical as the lead in pencils, but the atoms are arranged differently.

Every breath you take includes atoms once breathed in by any historical figure you can think of – Einstein, Henry VIII, Aristotle, Julius Caesar…

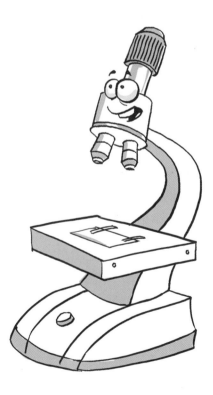

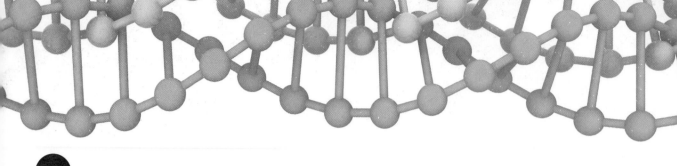

The slime produced by a slug produces a small electric current when smeared over copper. Slug-powered mobile phone, anyone?

The world's tallest limousine was built in Australia and measures 3.33 metres (10 feet 11 inches) from floor to roof. It took 4,000 hours to complete it.

An Australian scientist started a long experiment in 1927 to prove that *pitch* (a sticky black substance used for waterproofing boats and roofs) is not solid, but a very thick liquid. He put some pitch in a funnel and left it to drip through – by 1995, only seven drops had fallen through the funnel!

An American inventor has built a computer inside a stuffed, dead beaver.

A company in the USA has developed a luminescent computer keyboard which allows you to type in the dark!

Edwin A Shackleton (UK) has flown in 843 different types of aircraft. He reached this total in January 2007 and holds the world record.

Two American scientists have made a computer mouse that is fitted inside the skin of a real, dead mouse. Gross!

Pigeons won't land on a statue that contains the metal *gallium*. A Japanese scientist is developing a spray containing gallium that can be used to treat buildings to keep them free from bird droppings.

Diamonds sparkle because light reflects around inside them, bouncing off the inside of the faces.

Scientists in Italy are experimenting with a pill made from the same material as disposable nappies to help people lose weight. The pill expands to 1,000 times its original size in about 30 minutes, making the person feel full up, so that they don't eat. The effect lasts about two hours.

Plastic can take up to 500 years to decompose.

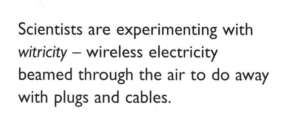

Scientists are experimenting with *witricity* – wireless electricity beamed through the air to do away with plugs and cables.

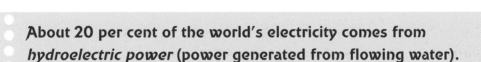

About 20 per cent of the world's electricity comes from *hydroelectric power* (power generated from flowing water).

The heat of chilli peppers is measured in *Scoville heat units*. The world's hottest chilli pepper is the *Bhut Jolokia* from India, at 577,000 units.

The first railroads were built in Germany around 1550.

At temperatures below about minus 25 degrees Celsius (minus 13 degrees Fahrenheit), bubbles can freeze in the air and shatter when hitting the ground.

One of the latest advances in technology is a *slugbot* – a robot designed to hunt down slugs!

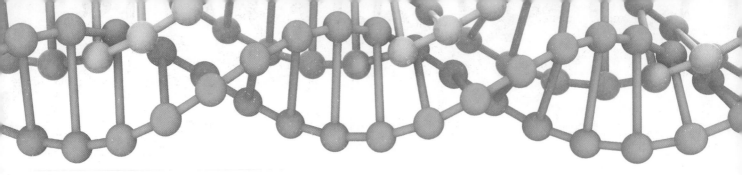

A ball of lead and a ping-pong ball would hit the ground at the same time if they were dropped inside a tube containing no oxygen.

Some types of rubber can be stretched to 1,000 times their original length.

An *android* (human-like robot) has recently been designed with light sensors behind its eyes, so it can follow a person's movements. There are others who can 'breathe', move and talk like humans.

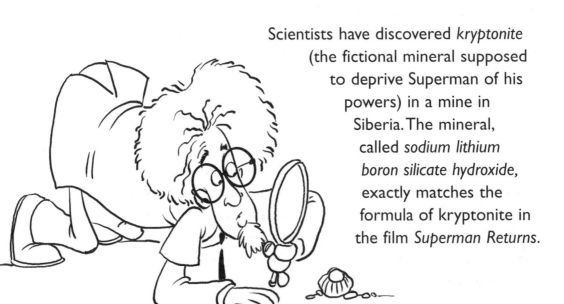

Scientists have discovered *kryptonite* (the fictional mineral supposed to deprive Superman of his powers) in a mine in Siberia. The mineral, called *sodium lithium boron silicate hydroxide*, exactly matches the formula of kryptonite in the film *Superman Returns*.

Using *nanotechnology* (technology at a very small scale, working with individual molecules) revolutionery new bullet-proof materials are being developed. They are so tough that bullets bounce off them! Someone wearing a jacket made with the new material will be completely unharmed if they are shot.

A mobile phone is being developed that can translate foreign languages. You take a picture of the text using the camera and then your translation will come through within seconds. Handy if you're lost for words on holiday!

Nicholas Joseph Cugnot designed the first car in France in 1769. It ran on steam and on rails!

In a magnetic material (such as iron) tiny groups of atoms line up, each with a north and south pole of their own, like miniature magnets.

Sound travels through air at a millionth of the speed of light, which is why you see lightning flash before you hear thunder.

A *smart toothbrush* uses wireless technology to send information to a screen that can be stuck on a bathroom mirror. The toothbrush monitors and reports back on how well you are brushing, and if you've missed any bits!

Aluminium is the most common metal on Earth, yet it never occurs naturally in its pure form – it's always found in combination with other chemical-making minerals.

The world's largest flat-screen television was unveiled in 2008, measuring a huge 3.81 metres (12.5 feet) diagonally from corner to corner.

French scientist Antoine-Francois Fourcroy had the lovely job of studying the effects of heat, air, water and other chemicals on rotting corpses.

Oxygen turns to a blue liquid at minus 183 degrees Celsius (361 degrees Fahrenheit). It freezes to a solid at minus 218 degrees Celsius (424 degrees Fahrenheit).

People have known that the lead in paint is poisonous since at least 1904 – but lead paint was still widely used until the mid-1960s.

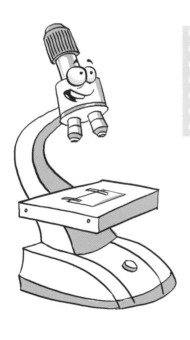

Scanning tunnel **microscopes are so powerful they can reveal individual atoms.**

Recycling ten drinks cans takes the same amount of energy as making one new one.

Phosphorous (the chemical used for making matches) was first created when chemists extracted it from their urine. The urine was left to stand until it *putrefied* (went bad). It was later extracted from burned and crushed bones.

The first computers used to be so big that they would take up a whole room! By the 1960s the electronic parts were getting smaller, so they gradually shrank in size. Today, computers can be so tiny they can fit inside your hand!

Sound travels faster in warm air than in cold air.

There are now robots that are so life-like that they can copy human expressions like smiling, sneering, frowning and squinting.

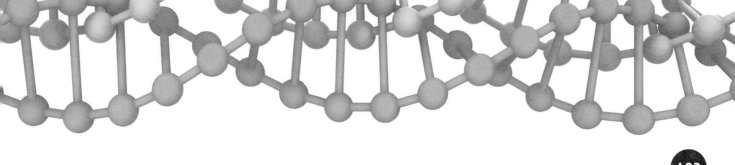

Optical fibres are extremely thin threads of glass. They can be used to carry cable television signals and in the tiny cameras used by surgeons.

Two billion atoms would fit on this full stop.

Any magnetic material that is touching a magnet starts to behave like a magnet too! If you attach a paper clip to a magnet you'll discover that you can attach another one to the first paper clip…then another… as many as you like! If you then break the first clip's contact with the real magnet they will all fall off and lose their 'stolen' magnetism!

Archaeologists have found what they think was a cream for treating pimples in the tomb of an ancient Egyptian prince.

The Burj Dubai in Dubai, United Arab Emirates, is still under construction, but is already the world's tallest freestanding building on land measuring 598.5 metres (1,964 feet) tall. When it is completed it's planned to be more than 800 metres (2,625 feet) tall! Not advisable if you're afraid of heights…

The water you get from the tap has been through many other people's bodies before it gets to you. But don't worry – it's been cleaned!

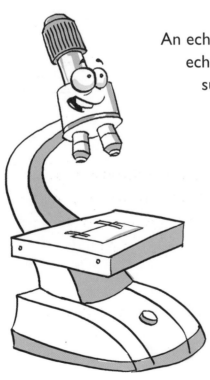

An echo is a sound reflection. To hear an echo, the sound must bounce off a surface that's at least 17 metres (56 feet) away. The echo still happens at closer distances, but it comes back too quickly for your ear to hear it.

Kodak introduced colour negative film in 1942.

The phrase 'in the limelight' meaning to be in the public eye comes from the bright lights used in theatres before electric lighting was invented. It was made by directing a flame at a cylinder of limestone, which would glow white-hot without burning or melting.

In 1896 in a factory in Massachusetts, USA, *Dureyas* cars became the first mass-produced cars ever made when a run of 13 were built.

A traditional old recipe for plant fertilizer consisted of rotten cow dung, ground up bones and dry blood. In fact, you can still get any or all of these from a garden centre to make your own. Or you could just buy a bottle of fertilizer...

Recycling one glass bottle saves enough energy to power a computer for 25 minutes.

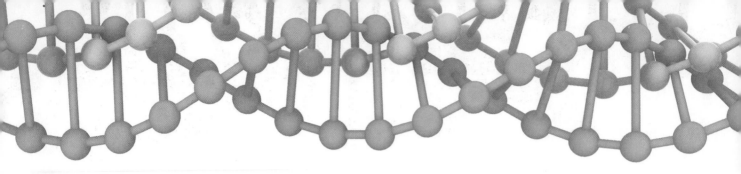

The world's largest solar energy roof is in the Netherlands and has an area of 26,110 square metres (281,045 square feet).

Scientists are trying to work out how to make signs that might be understood 10,000 years and more in the future to warn people of radioactive material that we are burying at the moment – it would be like us finding a message from Stone Age man!

The mould that gives Stilton cheese its special smell and flavour is related to penicillin, an antibiotic that you may take when you're ill.

Supersonic aircraft travel even faster than the speed of sound, which is about 1,220 kilometres (760 miles) per hour.

A Hungarian called Ladislo Biro invented the first ballpoint pen in 1938.

The first programmable computer, *Colossus*, was built in England during the Second World War to crack coded enemy messages. All 14 Colossus computers were destroyed after the war and the British government denied they had ever existed.

Scientists are trying to make *nanoswimmers* – tiny devices that can swim through blood vessels to keep people healthy or cure illness.

The largest nuclear weapon ever tested was the Russian *Tsar Bomba*, 1961. It had as much energy as a large earthquake, measuring 7 on the Richter scale.

An electronic air guitar device can pick up the movements of your pretend guitar playing and translate them into real guitar sounds.

Roads in Japan are being built with grooves cut in them so that if cars drive over them at the right speed they play a tune!

The biggest glass furnace produces more than 1 million glass bottles and jars every day.

Arsenic was so commonly used as a poison by murderers in the 1800s that a law was passed in Britain in 1840 that arsenic must be mixed with a blue or black dye so that people could see it in their food. It might have been better to stop pharmacists selling it…

Tall buildings are built not to wobble in the wind – but this isn't for safety, it's purely for comfort. People feel unsafe if they can see water sloshing around in the toilet!

Experimental *maglev* trains are able to run at up to 400 kilometres (248 miles) per hour. The trains aren't attached to the rails... they're just pulled along by magnetic force!

Tiny robots are used in microsurgery. They are so small they can fit inside your arteries.

A new way of paying for your shopping works by fingerprinting – the fingerprint is registered to bank details and people can pay just by showing a finger. Wonder if the finger has to be attached…

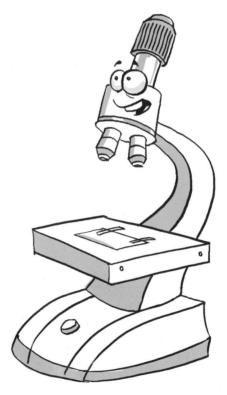

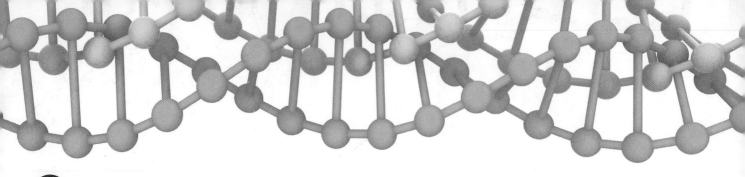

It takes 500 years for aluminium cans to break down – so recycle them!

Using a process called *plastination* to replaces body fluids with plastic, German doctor Gunther von Hagens preserves dead bodies and human organs. The real corpses are shown in art exhibitions and used as learning aids for training doctors.

The deepest hole ever dug by humans is in the Kola Peninsula in Russia – the drilling was completed in 1989. It was 12.3 kilometres (7.6 miles) deep.

If you dip a flower into liquid nitrogen it freezes instantly and becomes so brittle that you can smash it with a hammer.

It would take
**200 million flies to pull
a car at 64 kilometres
(40 miles) per hour.**

A *mirage* is an image of something that is not really there. It is caused by a layer of warm air over a layer of cold air – this bends the light making things that are really far away appear much closer than they really are.

A dentist from New York invented the electric chair.

Tom Thompson (USA) was pronounced dead, but emergency surgery saved him. He holds the world record for having the largest metal plate ever inserted into a human skull. Made of titanium, the plate measures 15 by 11 centimetres (5.9 by 4.33 inches).

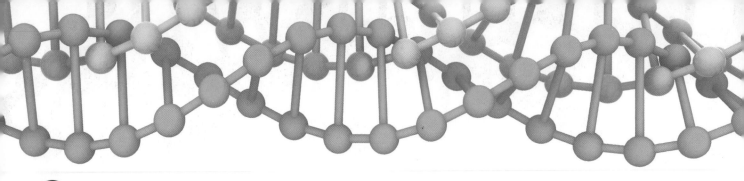

Some foods, including celery, use up more of your energy as you chew and digest them, than you can gain from eating them! In theory, you would actually lose weight the more celery you ate.

Electricity doesn't travel through a wire, but in a field around the wire.

The heaviest building ever to have been relocated while still intact is the Fu Gang Building in the Guangxi Province of China. It weighs 15,140 tonnes (33 million pounds) and is 34 metres (111 feet) tall. It was moved a total of 35 metres (115 feet) in 11 days.

If you mix corn syrup and tar together by stirring, you can separate them again by stirring in the opposite direction.

The first mechanical clocks were made in Europe in the 13th century. None of the first ones survive, but they're mentioned in church records from the time.

The Grand Coulee Dam that blocks the Columbia River, USA, is 20 metres (66 feet) taller than the Great Pyramid of Egypt.

Soap bubbles blown into air that is below a temperature of minus 15 degrees Celsius (5 degrees Fahrenheit) will freeze when they touch a surface. The air inside will gradually diffuse out, causing the bubble to crumple under its own weight.

John Logie Baird invented the television in 1926.

In 1996, General Motors, USA unveiled the *EV1* battery-powered car that sparked a new trend for eco-friendly vehicles. Electric vehicles were popular about 100 years ago until petrol use took over.

The world's 'cheapest' motorcar was unveiled in India in 2008. The *Tata Nano* is made by Tata Motors and will sell brand new for $2,500 (£1,277). It keeps the costs down by having no air conditioning, air bag, electric windows or assisted steering, and can only reach speeds of 70 kilometres (43 miles) per hour.

A raisin dropped into a glass of champagne will bob up and down continuously until the champagne goes flat.

If you put a drop of oil into a swimming pool, it spreads over the entire surface until it forms a really thin layer.

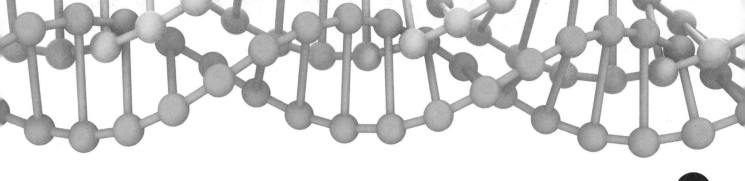

Alessandro Volta was an 18th-century scientist who developed the *voltaic pile* that later progressed into a battery. *Voltage* (the measure of current strength) is named after him.

In its usual form, antifreeze is deadly poisonous, but researchers in the USA are developing an edible form to make the perfect ice cream!

American researchers are working on a 'laser toothbrush' that zaps bad bacteria between the teeth with a blue-light laser beam. In just two minutes, your teeth would be squeaky clean all over!

Recycling just one tin can save enough energy to power a television for 3 hours!

The metal *gallium* melts at body heat – if you held a piece in your hand, it would gradually melt to a liquid pool.

A bowling ball needs to tilt by a 7.5-degree angle to fall over.

Over 10 million bricks were used in the construction of the Empire State Building, New York.

If you throw an aluminium can into a recycling bin, it can be recycled and ready to use again in just six weeks.

Joseph Gayetty (USA) produced the first factory-made toilet paper in 1857 – he was so pleased with his product that he had his name printed on every sheet!